# HUES OF LIFE

## A Book of Short Stories

# HUES OF LIFE

## A Book of Short Stories

**Syed Ibrahim Rizvi**

GenNext Publication

*Published by*

GenNext Publication
5, Ansari Road
Daryaganj, New Delhi-110002
Phone: 011-47034999, 9811692060
E-mail: gennextpublication@hotmail.com

*Distribution Network*
gyanbooks.com
India, USA, Canada, UK, Australia, France



ISBN: 978-93-5663-947-8 (PB)

"An Imprint of Kalpaz Publication"
First Published, 2023

*Printed at:* Gyan Press, Delhi.



**HUES OF LIFE: A BOOK OF SHORT STORIES**
Author: SYED IBRAHIM RIZVI

**This book is dedicated to**
**my father Late Agha Rizvi**
**who through his genes gave me the gift of**
**weaving thoughts into words**

## Acknowledgements

My first book '**A Kaleidoscope of Thoughts**' published in 2020 and the second book '**A Tryst with Emotions**' published in 2022 have been very well received by the audience. A huge number of well-wishers congratulated and encouraged me to continue my journey into literature. I acknowledge all my peers who have been eloquent in their praise for my short stories. I would be failing in my duty if I do not acknowledge the dedicated teachers of my first school, the Boys High School, Allahabad, who took pains to instill in me the subtlety of English language.

**Syed Ibrahim Rizvi**

# Preface

Biologically speaking, humans are no different from animals. We, as humans, share the basic biochemistry, physiology and anatomical features with most terrestrial animals. As evolution progressed the process of natural selection played a significant role in creating cognitive abilities and the brain got bigger. Humans as a distinct species evolved through this process with cognitive abilities which were much more advanced than their predecessors. The higher cognitive attribute gave humans the intellect to become masters of the planet. As a byproduct of our higher cognitive abilities, humans experience a wide range of emotions which play an important role in our behaviour which is termed as 'humane'.

Emotions provide humans with a host of attributes which make us so unique among all living creatures. Life is so beautiful only when we experience fear, anger, joy, sadness, disgust, and surprise. Another gift which humans got through the evolution of the brain was the ability to experience three dimensions: past, present and future. No other animal has the ability to remember the past, stay in the present and also foresee a future. It was therefore no surprise that humans evolved the ability to create fictional thought. To delve into a realm which is not real but made to look real, is an ability which is unique to humans.

The art of creating fictional stories have played a pivotal role all throughout the 2,00,000 years of the history of Homo sapiens. Fictional thought, in the form of stories, is universal and prevalent in all cultures and geographical regions of the world. The compilation of such human endeavors constitutes a very important pillar of human existence and is known as Literature.

The present book is a compilation of seven short stories which provide a glimpse of most human emotions including love, romance, empathy, belief, sorrow, joy and jealousy. The book would make an interesting companion for an audience with an interest in the English language.

**Syed Ibrahim Rizvi**

# Contents


Acknowledgements 7

Preface 9

1. Of Black Tuxedo and Maroon Sari 13
2. Pretty Girl in High Heels 29
3. The Don and the Damsel 41
4. A Tale of Two Generations 55
5. When Belief Came Crumbling 69
6. Why Did You Marry Me? 77
7. Shoot Out in Kamatipura 95

# 1

# Of Black Tuxedo and Maroon Sari

The fresher's induction programme was an anticipated annual event in the Management Institute of University of Allahabad. With the existing anti-ragging rules in place, the fresher's induction was the only event which provided an excuse to the seniors and juniors to break the ice.

Following the yester years norms, all the first semester students had been informed about the dress code for the anticipated event. The boys were expected to wear *kurta-pyjama* and girls had to wear a *sari*. Sumaira also saw the circulating notice about the dress code and started contemplating how she would convince her old-fashioned parents into allowing her to go out wearing a *sari*. Till date she had never worn one.

The function date came closer and hectic preparations were underway. Both the seniors and juniors were preparing various cultural items to be presented. The bonhomie belied the traditional cultural inhibitions of most of the students, the run up to the event sometimes provides more enjoyment than the actual function. Sumaira found the new atmosphere highly pleasurable. She had never interacted with boys in such closed groups. She realised there was so much excitement in life beyond the confines of her traditional upbringing.

After days of cajoling and requests, Sumaira's parents finally relented to allow her to attend the function wearing a *sari*. Sumaira took the help of an elder cousin to drape the *sari* and was ready much before she had to go to the function. A subtle application of lipstick and mascara was more than enough to make her face glow on that afternoon. With nineteen birthdays behind her, she looked stunning in that *maroon sari* with a bronze border.

The seniors had made all the preparation of the function. Javed was a live wire, he was good at studies and also took part in extracurricular activities. That evening in black tuxedo, he looked straight out of Hollywood. The evening started with formal speeches and extended into full blown cultural extravaganza. Javed mesmerised the audience with his solo song and drumming. The finale of the programme saw all seniors and juniors walking the makeshift ramp with montage music in the background. Sumaira also had an opportunity to get an eye full of Javed. She had seen him before but this afternoon she realised how talented Javed was. The overdose of adrenaline in her blood made her even prettier.

It was late evening that the function got over. Sumaira's silent mobile phone displayed several missed calls from her parents. At the first opportunity she called back to inform that she was on way back home. Walking out of the Institute, Sumaira re-arranged her *sari* and went to the main gate to find a rikshaw. She realised that the weather had taken a turn with cool breeze and dark clouds in the sky. Sumaira was still in her thoughts when the first drops of rain came. Within no time it started raining. The small shade at the gate provided scant protection to Sumaira from the downpour.

It was already dark and Sumaira had not yet been able to find a conveyance. Her thoughts were now focused more on the possible hostile reception at home than to the function where she had enjoyed the open atmosphere and the company of friends. Abstract in thought, she didn't notice the motorcycle which had stopped a few yards where she was standing. She heard a male voice call her name. Half drenched, Javed stood in front of her. With water dripping from his helmet, Javed's countenance beckoned Sumaira to sit on the motorcycle. Sumaira's upbringing had been strict, she had never been in such a situation. While Javed stood cleaning his helmet shield, a thousand thoughts crossed Sumaira's perplexed mind. She hesitated but an unknown instinct took over. Even before she could understand the repercussions, she found herself sitting on the pillion seat of the motorcycle.

While Javed navigated the motorcycle, Sumaira sat dumbstruck on the backseat. She realised Javed had not asked her the address. Perhaps Javed knew her house. She was finding it difficult to balance herself on the backseat but the thought of catching hold of Javed for support was too preposterous for her. She closed her eyes and started praying. Suddenly the motorcycle stopped. The deacceleration caused her to move forward, in a reflex to keep balance she had to grip Javed by the shoulder. She opened her eyes and found that Javed had stopped a good fifty yards from her house. Sumaira got down and started walking towards her home, after a few steps she looked back. Javed was looking at her, she gingerly waved at Javed and hurried towards her home.

Her mother was livid, in the drenched *sari* Sumaira felt extremely vulnerable. She didn't utter a word and went to her room. A silent prayer escaped her lips when no one pestered her to enquire how she had come back home despite the rains. From inside her room, Sumaira could overhear her father calming her mother and prodding her to ignore the episode. Sumaira felt relieved. That night her thoughts catapulted her to the events of the evening. Somehow every such thought ended with the memory of Javed and the journey back home.

The routine of classes started from the next Monday and Sumaira was hard pressed to find time for any gossip pertaining to the fresher's function. Intermittently she caught a glimpse of Javed or passed him in the corridor, but no words were spoken. A couple of times she sensed that Javed had fleetingly smiled at her acknowledging her gaze.

It was two weeks later while Sumaira was downloading something in the library that she realised she had company. Javed was on the adjoining computer. With a sheapish grin, Sumaira said 'Hi'. To her surprise, Javed was more forthcoming in his response. Javed engaged her in conversation which drifted from pleasantries to family background. After half an hour when Javed took leave to attend a lecture, Sumaira felt her cheeks getting hotter. She realised Javed had an infectious overbearance. Her hands felt cold and she breathed faster. Sumaira also had a class but she decided to skip it. Her mind was too intoxicated with Javed.

The next six months passed with Sumaira finding excuses to talk to Javed or stealing a few moments of his company. Twice she had found Javed at the gate of the Institute while she was waiting for a conveyance and had shown no reluctance to sit on the motorcycle.

A year had passed since Sumaira had enrolled in the MBA course and now, she had many friends. Recently news had percolated that one of her friends was getting married. Hurriedly all the batchmates had pooled money for the gift and most of the students had made preparations to attend the marriage. Sumaira found it extremely hard to convince her parents for permission to attend the marriage. She wept and showed her dissent. Despite her mother's stiff resistance, it was again her father who came forward to Sumaira's rescue. Sumaira got permission to go to the marriage function.

That evening, in dark green sequin dress, Sumaira looked an unblemished beauty. A year in the Management course had removed her inherent shyness. She was indeed pretty. The marriage function again gave Sumaira a chance to be in the informal settings with Javed within communicating distance. The photographer in attendance had taken many photos with Javed and Sumaira in one frame. Sumaira enjoyed the limelight.

It was already late when Sumaira took leave from the hosts. To her surprise Javed too announced that he was preparing to go home. Both of them walked towards the exit together. Without any obvious intent, Javed stopped his motorcycle in front of Sumaira with a look which was both inviting and benign. Sumaira hesitated but a surge of adrenaline made her choice easy. With a hand perched on Javed's shoulder for support, she settled on the pillion seat.

The sky was cloudy with few lights on the road as Javed rode his motorcycle at a speed which was a bit on the faster side. Sumaira was engulfed in thoughts which were alien. Twice she fought within herself a compelling impulse to put her hand across Javed. Deep in her thoughts, suddenly she realised that Javed had taken a detour which was not going to her house. After a minute into the new route, Javed stopped. With a curious expression Sumaira looked at Javed. The look on Javed's face belied any emotions, he informed that he wanted to get a jacket and therefore had come to his room. It was dark and the lane was lonely. Sumaira followed Javed to his room.

The brief visit to the room ostensibly to fetch a jacket took approximately forty minutes. She emerged from the room with a look which portrayed an expression of guilt. Sumaira's hair was disheveled and her appearance pale. Silently she took her seat on the motorcycle before Javed let go the accelerator on way to her home.

In the weeks that followed, Sumaira became recluse. She avoided eye contact with Javed when they passed each other. At home, her mother was perturbed at the change in behaviour of Sumaira. She missed her meals and seemed forlorn. Sumaira experienced constant headache. She wanted to go back in time and erase the moment when in an emotional frenzy she had consented to go to Javed's room.

A few days later, just as she had finished breakfast, Sumaira experienced a sudden bout of nausea. She also felt a strange kind of weakness which she had never experienced. The next day the spell of nausea came at lunch and her mother decided to check with a doctor. The doctor examined Sumaira carefully taking her vital parameters. After fifteen minutes, he asked Sumaira to go out of the room and taking her mother into confidence explained that Sumaira was pregnant.

Sumaira's mother was distraught. In her wildest dreams she could not imagine that Sumaira would do such a thing. The mood in the house was nothing less than an untimely demise. After a few days, discreetly, a veiled Sumaira was accompanied by her mother to a gynaecologist. The doctor wanted a high fees for medical termination of pregnancy. The procedure was over in a few days.

The immediate fallout of this unfortunate episode was that Sumaira's dream of completing an MBA was halted. Her father had also taken her mobile phone. Sumaira felt lonely and bewildered. The elders in the family had reached a consensus that Sumaira must be married as soon as possible. Despite the best efforts of the family, information had leaked within the extended family. Prying relatives were already debating the repercussions.

While Sumaira's life was taking an unexpected turn, another story was unfolding approximately 1300 kilometers away. Jabir had started sending feelers to relatives for seeking a second marriage proposal. It's been six months since his wife had died due to dengue. They had been married for four years and life was progressing smoothly until the untimely death of his wife. Jabir's only regret was that the couple had no children. Jabir had consulted the best doctors in Mumbai but nothing had succeeded. After his wife's death, Jabir had resolved that he would not marry again but six months later he had realised that life was a long journey and he needed a partner. He loved children and wanted to have a family.

Jabir's fortune was massive. The Al Jazain construction group had business ventures in the Middle East and Turkey. Despite his opulence, Jabir who was already on the other side of forty, knew, that it would be difficult to find a consenting family which would agree to marry their daughter to him. The yearning for a child was too strong for Jabir and he was ready to make any compromise for his second marriage.

When Sumaira's parents got a call from a distant relative proposing the marriage of their daughter to Jabir, they took very little time to give their consent. Sumaira was not consulted and a date was fixed. As a precaution to prevent rumour mills, the marriage was a low-key affair. Even Jabir, with a faint guilt of marrying within a year of his wife's death, wanted a modest celebration. A small emotional aberration, on that fateful Saturday, had resulted in Sumaira getting on the flight for Mumbai with a middle-aged Jabir as her husband.

Sumaira found it difficult to adjust in her new surroundings. Other than Jabir, she had no company in the lavish house. Despite all the luxuries, Sumaira found herself too lonely. Frequently in her thoughts she would find herself among friends at the Management Institute. At times, her thoughts wandered to the memories of time spent with Javed. Perplexing as it is, she seldom blamed Javed for the happenings of that Saturday night. Sumaira had long taken the blame on herself.

Time is a big healer. After a few months, Sumaira forgot her past travails and started to adjust to her new role as Jabir's wife. Jabir became fond of Sumaira and doted her, however he was always in the mental tension of his growing age. Jabir longed for a child. Two years had passed and Sumaira had not conceived. On a lazy afternoon, discreetly, Jabir opened up to Sumaira and proposed that both of them visit a doctor.

The doctor examined the couple and prescribed a series of tests before he reached a diagnosis. The process took several weeks. In one of the sessions, the doctor asked Jabir to visit the clinic alone in person. After a counselling session, the doctor in veiled language indicated to Jabir that there was no problem with his wife. In fact, it was Jabir who had a deficiency which was the cause of infertility. The information hit Jabir hard. Returning to his home he felt old and disinterested in life. He realised he would die without an heir. This thought was very depressing.

The Al-Jazain company was recruiting marketing and management professionals for their overseas operations. The recruitment team was visiting all major Universities for campus placement. Four MBA graduates were selected from Allahabad University, one of them was Javed.

Javed joined his new job in Mumbai. He had no idea of the owner of the Al-Jazain company. Some days later Jabir called a meeting of his newly recruited employees and interacted with them seeking details about their qualifications and past experience. Javed introduced himself as an MBA from Allahabad University. Jabir thought he had heard this name before. Without showing any outward emotion, his sharp mind went into overdrive. It was after the meeting that Jabir could make out the hiccup of his memory. He remembered that prior to his second marriage with Sumaira, he had heard something about Javed. A strange emotion engulfed his thoughts. On an impulse he was about to call the Head of the HR division to remove Javed but on second thought decided otherwise. He smiled.

Jabir told Sumaira that he would be inviting a very important guest tonight and that she should make appropriate preparations. The bell rang and Jabir asked Sumaira to attend to it. Jabir observed from a distance while Sumaira opened the door. For a moment Sumaira stared in disbelief, she stood paralysed not knowing how to react. Javed too looked aghast. A few seconds passed before Sumaira mustered the courage to make way for the visitor to step inside. Jabir observed the moment and his mind reaffirmed the rumours he had heard prior to his second marriage.

Jabir made his guest comfortable by diverting the conversation to matters concerning the affairs of the company. Sumaira had gone inside the house with a thousand thoughts, her mind was busy conjuring options if Jabir had any probing questions for her. Javed too was engrossed into introspection. He had never expected to come face to face with Sumaira in such a setting. Beyond this brief interlude, nothing of any consequence happened in the next thirty minutes. Without waiting for Sumaira to reappear, Javed took leave and left.

Javed and Sumaira both had a tough job at hand. Both, albeit in different setttings, were deep in thought trying to explain the events of this evening. Without an iota of doubt of any human involvement, both Javed and Sumaira blamed destiny for this strange coincidence. Jabir felt happy that his plan was taking shape.

Time passed. Javed became an integral part of the Al-Jazain company enjoying the confidence of the company's owner. It was a couple of weeks later that Jabir called Javed to his office and asked him to go to his residence and fetch some important papers. Javed found this errand a difficult one but showed no awkwardness in front of Jabir. He reached Jabir's residence and rang the bell. Sumaira had no idea about the person on the other side of the door as she opened it. Her heart skipped a beat. She lost her voice, she wanted to say that Jabir wasn't at home but no words came out, She moved away and allowed Javed to come inside. Javed explained that he had been sent by Jabir to fetch some papers. While Javed was about to leave with the papers that Sumaira regained composure to offer Javed a glass of water.

In the next few weeks, Jabir found trivial reasons to send Javed to his residence. Sumaira became used to such visits of Javed. At times she would smile when Javed would meet her sight. Her hesitation in striking a conversation also vanished after a few visits of Javed. She realised that Javed had not lost his sense of humour. Javed also realised that he looked forward to such errands which gave him an opportunity to interact with Sumaira.

Jabir perceived the unfolding events very closely by observing the behaviour of Sumaira. He realised that in the last few weeks Sumaira had become happier. Jabir was convinced his plan was working.

Jabir informed Sumaira that due to a business meeting he had to go to Delhi for a few days. He also informed his office of his impending absence from Mumbai. It was on the second day of Jabir's absence that Javed received a call from his boss at 10 pm. Jabir instructed Javed that he needed a few papers from his house and that he should go to his house and take those papers from his wife and then fax them at the given number.

Sumaira was startled by the ringing of the bell at such an odd time. She had already changed in night clothes. Sleepy eyed she opened the door. Finding Javed at the other side made her both happy and apprehensive. Javed, sensing her apprehension, told her about his boss's phone call. Sumaira let Javed inside the house. In that night dress, Javed found Sumaira amorously beautiful. Javed realised that in the last three years she had become more curvaceous. Sumaira met Javed's gaze. Her mind catapulted her to her first impression of Javed. He looked handsome. After serving Javed with a cup of tea, Sumaira went to her bedroom seeking to bring the papers.

Javed and Sumaira didn't realize they had spent forty minutes in each other's company.

After four days, Jabir checked out from his Mumbai hotel room and took a cab to his residence. At home he found Sumaira is a jovial mood. Life resumed without any change. Sumaira's mood profile changed to affable, Jabir was happy to observe her.

Sumaira felt giddy. This Monday morning she felt tired without any reason. A strange sensation gripped her. She felt confused. Later in the day she visited a doctor. The doctor took no time to break the good news to her. She returned home extremely happy. In the evening she tiptoed to meet Jabir at the gate and hugged him from behind. Such a show of affection was a rare sight in Jabir's life. In a soft husky voice, she whispered in Jabir's ears that she was expecting.

Jabir also showed happiness. Although he realised the reality, he became animated and hugged his wife. His face emanated a sly smile. Sometimes even losing self-respect can be joyful.

Time flew fast. Regular check-ups showed that the prospective mother and her child were doing fine. Jabir realised it was time to proceed to the next part of this unfolding story.

In the last few months Javed got only a few opportunities to meet Sumaira but every time it was in the presence of Jabir. He missed Sumaira and felt uneasy when rumors became rife that boss's wife was pregnant. All was going well when suddenly Javed got an office order that he was getting a promotion and was being posted in the Istanbul office of Al-Jazain company. He was expected to join within a week.

Jabir met his two guests discretely in his camp office. He had already neatly wrapped the two packets of US dollars which changed hands silently. The two guests left within a few minutes.

Javed was booked on Turkish airlines flight 717 leaving New Delhi at 6.15 am. While his colleagues felt jealous and thought Javed was being rewarded by the boss, Javed was feeling the pain of leaving India. He knew he would now not be able to meet Sumaira.

Javed had no idea that the two persons who were standing in front and back while he was passing through the security and customs were actually watching him closely. They were trailing him since he had entered the departure lounge of the IGI airport.

It was around 9 am local time in Istanbul when the flight TK 717 landed at the Istanbul airport. Passing through the duty-free shops, Javed observed the fine display of Turkish delights. Sleepy eyed, having not slept the whole night, Javed moved forward towards the security scanning. His baggage moved through the X-ray. The sensor bleeped. The man at the desk flagged his bag and asked Javed to come out of the line. Javed was taken to another room for questioning. Police officers took turns to interrogate. Javed was booked for carrying drugs in his hand bag.

The Paşakapısı Prison is a small prison located in Üsküdar district of Istanbul. This was going to be the address of Javed for the next five years after being found guilty of trying to smuggle drugs into Turkey.

Sumaira had no idea why Javed had not shown up for the last several months. She did not want to ask Jabir. In fact, it was Jabir himself who, as a passing comment, mentioned that Javed had gone to Turkey and had been arrested for carrying drugs. He expressed his empathy for Javed. Sumaira had no option but to believe what Jabir told her.

Sumaira was in the final trimester of her pregnancy. She felt depressed but Jabir made all the effort to make her happy. About two weeks premature, she delivered her baby. Finally, Jabir had a son whom he named Kamraan.

Taking care of Kamraan was a full-time job for Sumaira. She was always busy. Time flew fast. Kamraan's first birthday was celebrated with gaiety. Kamraan started to say a few words and take a few strides. It seemed a short time when time came to celebrate Kamraan's second birthday. Kamraan's looks were a sight to behold, he belied the dark complexion and shallow eyebrows of his father. Jabir found him cute.

Javed found the going tough in an alien prison. He started teaching English to his Turkish prison inmates. His affable nature and obedience were noticed by the prison authorities and they recommended that his prison sentence be condoned. It was to Javed's delight that on a Friday morning when he had just finished his prayers, the jail in-charge informed him that Javed would be freed on National Day of Turkey which was just a week later on October 29.

Kamraan's fourth birthday was just a week away. Sumaira was already indulging with all her gusto to celebrate this event. This year the guest list was larger. Despite his constant medical niggles, Jabir was also excited at the thought of Kamraan's birthday. In the last four years, he had all but forgot the Javed connection.

The birthday celebration had just started. The guests had assembled round the table which had the three-tier cake. The family was in attendance and Kamraan cut the cake. As everyone clapped, Jabir sensed his phone was vibrating. He did not want to pick the phone but when the vibration continued for an extended time, Jabir moved to a corner and picked the phone. The voice on the other side sounded somewhat known but he could not pin point the person. The man on the other side said only one sentence, 'Kamraan is my son and I am coming to take him'.

Jabir felt his hand go numb and pain in his jaw. The heaviness in his chest was so obvious that it was difficult to ignore. Javed understood his medical condition. He fished out the monosorbitrate drug which he kept in his pocket but his hands could not put that tablet where he wanted under his tongue. He choked and his knees gave way. People rushed to him but he became still before medical help could be provided.

Within six months of Jabir's death, Sumaira left Mumbai and moved to her ancestral town. In a small ceremony, a nikah was conducted with just a few relatives in attendance. Javed looked a perfect groom.

# 2

# Pretty Girl in High Heels

Her mother had neatly ironed her school dress late last night. Zeba was intensely adored and pampered by her parents. Today morning while Zeba was putting on the school uniform she felt a weird uneasiness. The knee length skirt somehow made her feel vulnerable and exposed. Her mind wandered to understand the reason for her averseness to the dress which she had been wearing for the last ten years but her eighty five billion neurons did not provide any answer. In an instant Zeba's thoughts deviated to the excitement of joining her friends in this new session of school where she will be a student of class XI.

Although Zeba had been a student of Benhur school for the last ten years, today she felt excited. She stood in the senior section line exclusively earmarked for the class XI and XII students. Her countenance also radiated her happiness of being the first position holder among girls in the just concluded ICSE examinations. While she stood in the line waiting for the school assembly to start, she silently nodded acknowledging the gestures of her friends which she perceived were due at her academic achievement.

Zeba's thoughts were punctuated by the sudden silence which heralded the presence of the school Principal on the dais. Mrs Simone was a petite character with a voice that exemplified a long career as a teacher. Without taking a moment, she opened the Book of Hymns and on rote started 'Our father, who art in heaven, hallowed be thy name............'. The students standing in columns dictated by their class, followed her words line by line. Abstract in her own thoughts, Zeba too followed the routine.

On usual days, the assembly would have dispersed after the prayer but today was the first day of the new session. Mrs Simone addressed the students extolling the virtues of being kind, obedient and honest. Some students paid heed or pretended to do so; some others bided their time. Mrs Simone did not pay notice to what the students did, she continued her prepared speech although speaking extempore. In the end of her address, Mrs Simone congratulated the students who had passed the board examinations and announced the names of the meritorious students. Zeba's heart raced when her name was called out being the first-place holder among girls. Amidst the din of the claps, she heard another name Jawed who got the first position among boys. Zeba and Jawed walked to the front and stood on either side of Mrs Simone. The students clapped in unison.

It was the second time that day when Zeba felt a tinge of shyness while she stood in front of the school assembly in that white and blue tunic and skirt. Some strange instinct made her feel embarrassed. She made a mental note that she will opt for the school uniform which provides covering to the full body.

Benhur school admitted both girls and boys, however, the sections were different, it was only in the XI and XII classes that both girls and boys shared a common class. Jawed was happy to be given so much attention in the assembly. By and large he was reticent in revealing his emotions but today it was difficult for him to hide his glee. Although he had seen that beautiful girl many a times during class breaks, today he came to know that her name was Zeba. Standing with Zeba, albeit with Mrs Simone marshalling the distance, Jawed found a strange pleasure filling his thoughts. It was in this backdrop that both Jawed and Zeba felt a bout of excitement when they realised that both were in the same section.

In the academic journey of any individual, classes XI and XII are the toughest. There is a quantum jump between the standards of X and XIIth class. Zeba also realised this hard fact quite early. She was always burdened with work and had the lingering burden of living up to others' expectations in view of her stupendous performance in previous board examinations. She realised that Jawed was very bright, invariably he was always the first one to answer questions in the class. Although direct communication was still far too infrequent, Zeba harboured a silent admiration for Jawed.

Besides acknowledging her intelligence, Jawed found Zeba an attractive girl. There was something in her which was infectious. For no obvious intention, Jawed found himself fabricating trivial reasons to court Zeba in conversation. Jawed's mind, however, was still baffled why he had developed a longing for Zeba.

Benhur School every year celebrated its annual day on July 5. This year was no different. The school administration had informed the students about the forthcoming festivities. Students from every class had prepared cultural programmes for the event. The school administration had given the responsibility of anchoring the event to Zeba and Jawed.

As part of the run up to the upcoming event, there were numerous situations when Jawed interacted with Zeba. After a few awkward episodes, Zeba found Jawed to be a good-mannered shy boy. Jawed too looked forward to his practice sessions with Zeba.

The Annual day had arrived, the guests were taking their seats. The dais was shielded by the heavy curtain. Jawed and Zeba, still seated in the green room, were ready to take their place before the mike once the curtain was raised. These were anxious moments. Both Zeba and Jawed were busy replaying their lines in their mind. The minutes passed very slowly, Jawed glanced towards Zeba, he realised she looked pretty in those black trousers and white shirt with loose tie. Jawed's sight caught a glimpse of her feet which sported a silver anklet and the golden thin strapped high heels. He realised that as part of the school uniform girls always wore black shoes. For a moment his eyes got transfixed to those lovely feet in high heels. Zeba's basic instinct prompted her that she was being looked at. She looked towards Jawed. As if on cue, she asked 'Jawed what are you thinking'. Jawed, with his eyes still riveted to the anklet sitting softly on the delicate feet, said in a soft voice 'your feet are beautiful'. Zeba's gaze met Jawed's sheepish eyes. She blushed. The clock struck 2, someone entered the green room and signaled to Jawed and Zeba. The curtain was raised and the annual function started.

Zeba and Jawed lived upto their academic reputations in the Class XI annual examinations. Jawed got the first position with Zeba on the second spot. Class XII was even more hectic than Class XI. Most of the students had joined additional coaching classes and were preparing for competitive examinations. Jawed had also enrolled for a reputed coaching and his attendance in the school became erratic.

Academic preoccupations played heavily on both Jawed and Zeba. Time flew fast, the class XII examinations were round the corner and the students skipped classes to prepare for the board and other competitive examinations. The extreme pressure of studies provided no time for students to divert their attention to friendships. In due course Jawed and Zeba also lost touch.

Jawed qualified the JEE examination and got enrolled for a B Tech course at a college in Hyderabad. Losing the comfort of home coupled with demands of the course left Jawed with little time for himself. His new friends provided the solace to his needs for extra academic endeavours. Zeba became just a relic of his memory.

Zeba's life had fewer twists and turns. After passing the class XII board examination, her parents were of the view that it was not advisable for Zeba to go to another city. Zeba got admission into the undergraduate course at Allahabad University. She too found new friends and within no time forgot the days spent at Benhur school.

Three years is a small time for a teenage girl enjoying the relaxed atmosphere of university life after a grueling twelve years of convent discipline. Zeba passed undergraduate and got herself admitted to master's course in Psychology. On the academic front, while Zeba was learning the theories of Sigmund Freud and Jean Piaget, nature was also playing its role in making Zeba fulfil the purpose of life. Zeba looked prettier than ever. Her perfectly chiseled physique made her stand out from her peers.

While Zeba was still in university, marriage proposals come flooding to her parents. Her parents had discretely tried to read Zeba's mind regarding her inclination. Zeba was steadfast in her stand, she wanted to finish her studies first.

Her parents therefore put on hold any marriage plans till Zeba completed her M.A.

Zeba did exceedingly well in final examinations. It was just fifteen days past her examination result that one evening her mother confronted her with biodata and photographs of three boys. Ostensibly Zeba didn't react. Although she shared a very friendly relationship with her mother but discussing a future mate in an open conversation was too preponderous. Zeba's mother realised her daughter's discomfort and left the room leaving the photographs and the biodata with Zeba.

Even in solitary setting, Zeba found a strange awkwardness in looking at the photographs and the details. In times of digital manipulations, every photograph looked straight from a glossy fashion magazine. The biodata also provided no clear understanding of the answers which Zeba's brain wanted in its endeavour to fulfil the evolutionary instinct of mate selection. After the initial cursory look, Zeba went through the profiles again. Her eyes caught sight of one photograph which ignited a far-fetched memory deep inside her brain. Despite an unfaithful faint resemblance, Zeba could not piece together why her mind singled out this photograph. She went through the biodata and realised that the boy was three years older than what she was. The boy was self-employed and had a big business. They lived in an adjoining city. It was on the third attempt that Zeba's mind retrieved the memory and she recollected that the photograph with the biodata lying before her on the bed was of Amir, who almost two decades back used to go on the same rikshaw to school while Zeba was in lower classes. A faint smile crossed her lips. She started recollecting how they used to fight for the best seat on the rikshaw. Amir evoked fond memories.

Subsequent formalities did not take time. The marriage was fixed and hectic preparations started. With age on her side and the excitement of marriage, Zeba looked a beautiful princess. There were many pre-nuptial festivities. The *haldi* ceremony was underway. Friends and relatives, as part of the custom, were applying curcumin paste on hands and feet of Zeba. With eyes half shut due to a myriad of strange emotions, Zeba was enjoying the moment. Someone straightened her legs and exposed her ankle. Zeba's eyes caught sight of her feet bathed in turmeric water. She closed her eyes, out of nowhere a memory flashed before her closed eyes. *She was sitting with Jawed in the green room waiting for the curtain to rise. Jawed said 'your feet are beautiful'.* Zeba's mind replayed the memory, the ensuing cacophony inside her mind and outside made Zeba to open her dreaming eyes. She realised her friends were singing in chorus the Sapna Awasthi wedding song '*banno teri ankhiyan….*'.

Zeba was married a few days later in a glittering ceremony. In golden *sherwani* and sporting a stubble beard, Amir looked dapper. Zeba wore an embroidered designer *lehnga* and in those pencil high heels encasing *henna* highlighted feet, she completed the perfectly blended married couple. With tears in the eyes of her parents, Zeba departed to her new abode.

Almost a thousand kilometers away in Hyderabad a new beginning was being scripted in the life of Jawed. After successfully completing his B Tech course he had joined a few small enterprises but continued his efforts for a government job. Today he received an email which brought him joy, a rare commodity in his life ever since he had lost his parents in the COVID wave the preceding year. He read the email several times, not that he did not understand its contents but because the contents gave him a reason to be happy. The email said that Jawed was being appointed as an Engineer in Konkan

Railway and that he had to report at the Headquarters in Vasco de Gama in fifteen days.

The job in Konkan railway was professionally very satisfying for Jawed. Voluntarily he would work extra hours. One reason for his dedication was also because he had few distractions. While colleagues coaxed him to enjoy the Goan nightlife, he was contended to stay in his flat with books as his companion.

A month had passed while Jawed had been in Goa but he had not yet been to the famed beaches of the land. He made a mental note that on the next weekend he would take a taxi and visit the Calangute beach in north Goa.

Zeba was enjoying every bit of her married life. She was extremely pampered by her in-laws. While Amir was constantly busy with his business engagements, it was the insistence of his parents who had put their foot down to make Amir take a break and plan a honeymoon with Zeba. The couple decided that the best destination would be Goa. Flights and hotel were booked. With dreams in her eyes, Zeba embarked upon the journey to her honeymoon, recollecting all those stories from Mills and Boon which she had read as a teenager.

It was Saturday morning, Jawed woke up late. He had slept long on this weekend. Even at 10 am his eyes wanted to go back to the dream which he was experiencing some time back. In dream, Jawed had gone back in time when his father took him to Benhur school for admission as a toddler in KG. In the next moment he found himself playing cricket with friends. He vividly dreamt of the Benhur Annual function which he anchored with Zeba. While Jawed lay in bed lazily on that October Saturday morning, his mind went into slideshow of events of the past. He wanted to pause the slideshow while his mind reached Zeba's timeline. The phone rang and the taxi driver announced that he would be coming in an hour. Jawed jumped from the bed and started getting ready.

It was already night when Amir and Zeba checked into the luxury Le Meridien Goa near the Calangute beach. After dinner they decided to have a stroll, the smell of sand and sea was already in the air when they stepped out of the hotel. All roads pointed out to Calangute beach which was just a few hundred meters.

After a lazy breakfast at the hotel, the next day, Amir and Zeba decided to visit the famous Calangute beach. Amir changed into a Bermuda while Zeba slipped into a yellow t-shirt and loose jeans. They decided to walk to the beach.

Jawed reached the Calangute beach just before afternoon. The beach was crowded with motley visitors. A group of youngsters, probably part of a school excursion group, were playing beach volleyball. Interspersed in the crowd were many couples in various age brackets. It was not difficult to spot the honeymooners, unabashedly they threw caution to the winds while expressing emotions. There were others who were middle aged, sitting quietly hand-in-hand listening to the sound of waves. Jawed aimlessly walked at the edge of the water. The sand was now getting hot. He got bored. The hot sun had made him thirsty and he decided to visit one of the restaurants just opposite the beach before moving on to another beach in north Goa.

The far table at the *Tropicana Drink House* offered a good view of the beach. Jawed ordered a lemonade and sat, his eyes following the sea waves in their synchronised dance on the sandy beach. Jawed realised this motion of waves was timeless, it must have begun billions of years back when the earth came into existence. Legions of mankind have viewed this natural phenomenon in awe, mesmerised by the beauty of the water and serenity. Through the glass walls, Jawed saw a couple walking towards the restaurant. His eyes again wandered towards the natural beauty. The second time his sight caught the couple, he felt as if his mind was searching for some lost memory. The couple was now at the door of the restaurant. Jawed recognised the girl. Even in those large sun shade eye glasses she was unmistakably Zeba. Jawed missed a heartbeat.

The new couple took a seat in the other corner of the restaurant. It was apparent that they were newly married. The girl sported bright *henna* on her hands extending upto the forearms. Jawed realised that Zeba had grown into a beautiful girl, although she was fuller than what his memory had in store, her face radiated the same infectious attraction which Jawed felt when he stood with her on the stage anchoring the annual function at Benhur school. Without reason Jawed's gaze moved down to her feet. The fine grains of yellow sand sticking on the wet feet also could not hide the attraction of the *henna tattooed* beautiful feet, Jawed noticed the silver anklet on her right feet. Jawed felt his adrenal gland was pumping an overdose of adrenalin.

Jawed continuously looked towards Zeba trying to meet her eye when she looked towards him. Zeba, as part of her conversation with her husband, did intermittently look towards Jawed but her countenance showed no signs of acknowledging any acquaintance. Jawed was perplexed, his mind was still in denial with the fact that Zeba would not recognize him even in such close proximity.

Although the distance between the tables was such that it was difficult to overhear but Jawed sensed that Zeba and her partner were about to leave. Jawed saw Zeba take out a few papers and an assortment of cards from her bag. She wrote something on a piece of paper then put the papers again in her bag. Nobody paid any heed, but Jawed's eyes caught the sight of a small paper falling on the floor while Zeba stuffed other papers in her bag. Jawed's second lemonade was about to finish. He saw the couple pay the bill and leave the restaurant.

While Jawed paid the bill and moved towards the exit, he passed the table where a couple of minutes before Zeba was sitting. His eyes hit upon a piece of paper lying upside down below the table. Jawed hesitated but on second thought could not resist picking that piece of paper. It was a hotel address card of Le Meridien. On top of the card someone had written "Amir Siddiqui, room # 305".

Zeba's mind was getting confused. She was still not sure whether she should have acknowledged Jawed in that restaurant. She had recognised Jawed as soon as she had entered the restaurant, she also knew that Jawed was continuously looking at her. All during her stay in the restaurant she was conscious of Jawed's presence, her decision to remain oblivious was dictated by the presence of Amir. Zeba was uncertain how Amir would react to Jawed. Zeba debated within her mind whether her action of dropping the hotel card was a correct gesture.

It was dinner time, Amir and Zeba had a wonderful candlelight dinner. It was while they were having dessert that Amir received a phone call from home. Listening to the call he turned pale. The call was certainly not a positive sign. Amir told Zeba that father has had a heart attack and that they needed to reach their city as fast as possible. The hotel managed to get the booking on the first flight from Goa to Varanasi next morning. Amir and Zeba checked out of Le Meridien early morning and boarded the flight back home.

Jawed also could not sleep. Zeba's memory kept haunting him. Before he dozed off, he had already seen that Le Meridien card a hundred times. He debated a thousand options why Zeba had discretely given him a clue to her place of stay. If indeed she did want to meet him, she could have acknowledged his presence at the restaurant itself.

Compared to Saturday, Jawed did not sleep long the next day. He woke up still confused. All his academic achievements failed to provide him an answer to his current situation. Without any outward reason, Jawed got ready and hired a taxi to the Le Meridien hotel. It was 9 am at the reception when Jawed reached the hotel. His steps were heavy and speech a notch better than a slur. In a tone alien to his ears, Jawed asked the receptionist whether he can meet one Mr Amir Siddiqui booked in room # 305. Professionally the receptionist typed a few strokes on the computer and told Jawed that Mr Amir and his wife had already checked out early morning. Jawed felt a bout of melancholy. Although he knew Zeba was already happily married, a strange instinct made him yearn to meet her. Jawed was about to leave the reception counter when the receptionist asked him whether he was Mr Jawed. Without understanding the reason for this question, Jawed said 'Yes'. The receptionist handed him an envelope saying that Mrs. Amir Siddiqui had left this envelope while checking out. She had instructed that if Mr Jawed comes to the hotel, the envelope may be given to him.

Jawed, with a thousand emotions swirling in his mind, took the envelope and walked out of the hotel. He found a secluded spot under a tree. Gingerly Jawed opened the envelope. Inside the envelope there was a silver anklet and a piece of paper on which somebody had written "SORRY".

# 3

## The Don and the Damsel

The office was as usual bustling, this day the 30th of November was no different to other office staff that were in the process of settling down on their designated desks for the next eight hours of arduous public dealing. Salim took his seat and put his water bottle and lunch box in the creaking drawer of the wooden table in the same way as he had been doing for the last forty years. For a moment he became so engrossed in the files pending on his desk that he forgot that this was his last day in office. While he took out his pen from the pocket, Salim caught a sight of his new shirt which his daughter Hera had coaxed him to wear on the day of his retirement.

Except a few affectionate glances and winks from his aging friends, nothing unusual happened in the office while Salim went through the files. It was during the lunch break while he spread the old newspaper on his table to put the lunch box, Salim's mind momentarily drifted to that cold January morning forty years back when he had joined as a junior clerk in this office. His mind continued to wander while he munched his routine lunch pack of two rotis and a staple vegetable mix. A kaleidoscope of thoughts razed past his mind refreshing forty years of memories which were both fond and painful. He remembered the day when he lost his first wife due to dengue. The next moment his memories catapulted him to his second marriage to a distant cousin precisely twenty-five years back. A faint smile crossed his parched lips when his mind stumbled upon the memory of the birth of his daughter some twenty-two years back. Salim's train of memories was broken when the peon put a fresh bundle of files on his desk. Salim realised there were tears in his eyes, he took a mouthful of water from the bottle and once again settled down to finish the files. While he glanced on the other desks, he realised life was normal for other colleagues.

While the office gate closed at five in the evening, Salim realised that all the office staff had converged in the office of the Superintendent. A couple of his colleagues escorted Salim to the place where the other office staff was standing. A thin film of tear covered Salim's eyes. He didn't see for sure who placed the rose garland around his neck. The Superintendent was speaking something which pertained to extolling his long service to the office. The makeshift function lasted fifteen minutes. Salim glanced, for the last time, towards his chair which will have a new occupant tomorrow.

His wife and daughter were at the door of the house to welcome Salim. Although both daughter and wife realised the pain of retirement which Salim would be undergoing but Hera had made an effort to put a spirited show of exuberance to celebrate her father's retirement. The dinner was laid out with Salim's favourite *biryani*. That night Salim found the reality of retirement a difficult task to handle. His mind fumbled time and again to the forthcoming financial hardships. It was around midnight that Salim spoke to his wife about the proposal to rent out a portion of their house. He reasoned that this will in a way offset the financial hardships post retirement.

Salim's house was in the lane adjacent to the ICICI Bank. A few days later when he visited the bank, Salim put a word to some of the employees that there was a vacant space in his house which he wanted to rent out. Javed had recently joined as Assistant Manager at the ICICI Bank and was searching for a suitable place to live in the vicinity of the Bank. The Branch Manager told Javed about the availability of the accommodation at Salim's place in the adjacent lane. Javed made a mental note to visit Salim's house in the evening.

It was dusk and Salim was preparing to go to the mosque for the evening prayers. The doorbell rang while he was still in the final stages of ablution ritual, Salim called Hera to check out at the door. Hera was in the midst of kneading the flour when she heard the doorbell. With sticky dough on her hand, she draped the shawl around her shoulders and opened the door. Finding an unknown person made Hera conscious. Involuntarily she checked her drape and looked at the stranger with inquisitive countenance. Javed's eyes met her gaze. In that unkempt demeanor Hera looked innocently ethereal. For a moment Javed lost his reason, his basic instinct egged him to savour this moment. While Hera stood on the other side of the door with an enquiring gaze, Javed fumbled to find words to ask whether this place belonged to Mr Salim and that he wanted to meet him, if possible.

Salim found Javed to be a well-mannered boy with decent antecedents. He was willing to pay the rent without any haggling. The deal was finalised and Javed left Salim's house with a new address and a lingering memory of flour smeared dazed damsel.

The demarcation in the house was such that Javed had full privacy from Salim household. It was a rare moment when he would get a glimpse of Hera. Life moved on. Salim had settled into his retired lifestyle. On a couple of occasions, he did invite Javed for dinner but the middle-class religious upbringing never made Hera to come in front of Javed or to strike a conversation. Despite her discomfiture in meeting Javed with any direct eye contact, on occasions when she did glance at Javed she found him good – looking.

Javed found the family of his landlord affable. Salim and his wife on occasions offered home cooked food for Javed. It was a Monday morning when it started to rain heavily. Javed was getting ready to go to the bank when he suddenly found Salim knocking at his room. Salim looked worried. He told Javed that Hera had to take a competitive examination today and that with heavy rains and water logging she was not getting any public conveyance. Salim implored Javed to take Hera to the examination center on his motorcycle.

Both Javed and Hera were conscious of each other. Despite the exigency of the moment, Javed felt an unknown excitement while he drove to the examination center in that soft drizzle. At times Hera felt her hands clutching Javed, albeit involuntarily, in an effort to balance herself when the motorcycle waded through water logged streets. Even with a profound effort not to let her mind wander to the tune of evolutionary instinct, Hera found it impossible to distract her mind from sensing the warmth of Javed's body in that wet atmosphere. Today she felt an emotion which was alien to her until now. She felt happy.

While an innocent admiration was brewing between two individuals, just half a kilometer from Salim's house a lavish party was underway to celebrate the election victory of Jabir in the State assembly elections. The new MLA was entertaining his guests with all the vices available to humans. The guest list included, among others, every known criminal of the town.

After all, this was the occasion where politics was having a rendezvous with crime.

After becoming an official lawmaker, thanks to the modern definition of democracy, Jabir found it very easy to break law for sundry reasons. In the next six months he controlled all the liquor shops, sand mining leases and development tenders. Jabir's writ ran across the town, few had the courage to defy his diktat.

While Jabir's fortunes were spiraling in the new role of an elected representative, his marital life was giving him troubles. Jabir's flashy lifestyle and his love for extra marital flings had become a reason for divorce which his wife was seeking through a court notice. All his efforts to browbeat the petition had been in vain. The eminent separation with his wife had happened. Given his clout Jabir was in no way dependent on marital status to seek contentment, however, he felt he needed to show himself as a family man for popular public perception. Recently Jabir had received feelers from several quarters about beautiful girls whom he might consider marrying.

Someone close to Jabir had spoken to him about a beautiful girl who was the daughter of a retired government servant and lived near the ICICI bank just a few hundred meters away. Within no time Jabir had the biodata of the girl in question. Jabir found out that the girl belonged to a lower middle-class family with just old parents as guardian. The girl's image perfectly suited Jabir's quest for a showpiece wife with a meek background who would not object to his other interests.

It was Saturday and a day off for Javed. He was coming out of his room when he saw two white Toyota Fortuner cars stop at the door of his landlord. In the last six months Javed had got a fair idea of visitors at Salim's place. The arrival of Fortuner cars with unknown guests was something new.

Salim didn't recognize the guests either although he threw open the door to let the guests inside. Salim noticed that only the female guests had come out of the cars, there were some people in the other car who didn't come out and remained seated. The female guests were in expensive clothes and were ostensibly carrying a few gifts. Salim's wife was also perplexed but played host with all humility. The conversation meandered between normal exchange of pleasantries and everyday life. It was after about thirty minutes that the elderly lady in the visiting group dropped the question of Hera's marriage to Jabir. Hera's mother was not prepared for such a question. She had no answer, however, she did get an inkling that the tone of the proposal was not in the form of a question but as a foregone conclusion.

Although Salim had never met Jabir but he knew him as an influential MLA who commanded respect by his unlawful acts. The events of this evening had been frightening for the family. Salim realised that he was caught between the devil and the deep sea. Marrying Hera to Jabir was tantamount to mortgaging his daughter to an environment of crime and deceit.

Events happened fast from the time the unknown visitors had come to Salim's place. Almost everyday there was a flurry of activity with expensive cars and equally bejeweled visitors visiting Salim's house. Amidst the din of high-profile visitors, Salim's wish and voice had no influence. He was just a spectator to a proposed marriage of his daughter to the most dreaded man in the locality.

Hera was treated like a princess by Jabir after marriage which was a grand affair with the elite of the town in attendance. The constant flow of visitors and the new responsibility of being presentable made Hera so busy that she lost her hitherto constant contact with her parents. It was a good couple of months later that Hera started to feel pangs of loneliness in the sprawling mansion which now seemed suffocating. Despite being bathed in indulgence, Hera felt that she had to seek permission to go out even to her parental house. On rare occasions when she went outside, she was accompanied by security.

Time passed; the initial euphoria of marriage waned. Hera was now realising the reality of Jabir's life. Every day she overheard conversation between her husband and his associates which spoke of murder, abduction and crime. Hera grew restless. At times she got a feeling that Jabir was indulging in extra marital relationships. She realised that she was being treated as a namesake wife who was just a prisoner. Hera was now not allowed to meet her parents. She had lost all touch with them.

A year had passed for Salim since he last saw Hera. Aging has been fast after retirement. Salim and his wife were now perennial patients. At times Salim thought how lucky he was to have Javed as a tenant. Javed was always at hand to help Salim manage his post retirement niggles. Javed too felt a void after Hera's marriage. On numerous occasions he had to console his mind to distract it from the fond memories of Hera. At times he found himself cursing his shyness for not being able to muster the courage of talking to her. Forlorn in thought, he would frequently remember his feelings when Hera sat on the pillion of his motorcycle. It was well past midnight that Javed's mind prompted a plan. He started contemplating. Taking on Jabir was akin to challenging Goliath, but he knew to get Hera he had to become David.

Jabir's mansion was under security 24x7. The gate was manned and Jabir had issued clear instructions that both entry and exit was to be checked. It was Sunday morning when Javed reached the vicinity of Jabir's house. The mansion was the last house on the road before a dead end. A few roadside shanties dotted the path. Javed stopped at the tea vendor and ordered a tea. He saw a barber shop and a sweetmeat shop nearby. At the far end he could see the big green gate with embossed insignia of MLA.

The following week passed with Javed contemplating options. When Saturday came, he again went to the lane which led to Jabir's house. On this occasion, Javed took a seat in the barber shop keeping an eye on the house at the end of the road. He realised that there was very little traffic on the road, a few big cars did find their way inside the gate. Other than these sporadic occasions, the gate was mostly closed with two security guards. Today Javed spent a couple of hours biding his time in the barber shop and then sipping two cups of tea. It was just before noon, while he was preparing to go back to his room, that Javed saw a man walking upto the MLA house. The man carried a shoulder bag and he did speak to the guard about something. Javed saw the guard going inside. A couple of minutes later, Javed saw a woman come up the gate and receive a packet from the man who was carrying the bag. From the brief glimpse Javed could recognize Hera. The gate closed. Javed waited for the man to return. When he saw the man from close quarters, Javed recognised that he was a postman.

Javed's plan started to find substance. He played back the events and his observations of the Saturday morning. The postman was a big clue. His mind again reminisced about Hera. From a far recess of his mind, a memory of Hera became alive. He recollected that on an occasion when he had visited the inside of Salim's house on a dinner invitation, he had seen a shelf full of Urdu novels and periodicals.

The next Saturday, sporting a worn-out Khaki uniform and a tilted cap, Javed walked gingerly towards Jabir's house with a shoulder dangling bag full of packed envelopes and packets. He reached the gate where one of the sleepy guards accosted him. Javed had already played this scenario many times in his mind. He explained to the guard that a registered parcel had come for Mrs Hera Jabir. The guard silently walked inside the gate asking the postman to wait. It took an unusually long time for someone to respond. Javed's heart was pumping blood twice its capacity. His adrenaline was in over drive. After five minutes Javed saw the gate open. Hera emerged looking disillusioned and bored. She looked towards the postman. The postman handed her a packet. Hera's eyes caught a glimpse of the postman, her more than 80 billion neurons in the brain searched to piece together where she had seen this postman before. She found the answer, her eyes met Javed's gaze. Hera's memory went back almost three years back while she had stared, with disheveled looks, at a stranger who was standing at the door. The postman fished out a paper and pen and asked Hera to sign. Hera signed but didn't miss the note written on the paper "read page 50".

Hera experienced a tsunami of emotions. While she was happy to see Javed approach her, her knowledge of the reach and capability of Jabir was too intimidating. She started to think about Javed's safety. In the comfort of her room Hera unpacked the book. It was a monthly edition of a popular Urdu language magazine. Nothing unusual. She remembered the postman's note about page fifty. She glanced at page 50. Two printed pages had been inserted in the magazine at pages 50 and 51. She started reading what was written in those pages. The contents brought mixed feelings to Hera's mind. The plan looked feasible and achievable but if gone wrong the repercussions could be equally disastrous. That night she didn't sleep. When Jabir saw an Urdu book at the table, he inquisitively flipped it but couldn't understand its content. He spared a moment to glance at the pictures of girls in pretty dresses but paid no heed to the content.

Javed returned to his room excited. Seeing Hera after such a long time evoked fond memory. He realised he loved Hera. He again cursed himself for not expressing his love for Hera when she was not married. That night he didn't sleep peacefully. Thoughts of Hera and the next part of the plan punctuated his disturbed and erratic sleep. He made a mental note of things to do on Sunday.

The next day Javed called his old friend Atul who had a clinic in the old city. He fixed an appointment with him. From his friend Javed got the telephone numbers of few drivers who were operating ambulances. He contacted each one and then visited them. Manoj was in his fifties, he had long known Dr Atul and frequently ferried his patients. When Javed approached Manoj and explained his work, Manoj became jittery. Albeit politely, Manoj refused Javed. Two other ambulance drivers were approached but none showed courage to say yes to Javed's proposal.

Javed found himself losing the plot. He decided to take another chance. The next day Javed went to a used automobile store which had several dilapidated vehicles waiting for a prospective buyer. Moving through the long line of dirt laden assorted collection of vehicles, Javed found an ambulance. He negotiated the price of the ambulance and purchased it. The owner was also happy since such vehicles usually went unsold.

Javed spent a few thousand rupees to get the vehicle in running condition. He paid no heed to the other gadgets or to the worn-out tyres. He knew he required this vehicle for a specific purpose, there was no need of any medical equipment.

While Javed was busy preparing for his plan, Hera was constantly coaxing her mind to pump more courage in her heart to execute the plan which was explained on page 50 and 51 of the Urdu magazine.

This Saturday morning was no different in Jabir's mansion. Jabir had woken up early and completed his exercise and yoga routine according to everyday schedule. Today he was to address a public function in the forenoon. Later he was slated to meet the District Magistrate in connection with a few cases of land grabbing which Jabir's adversaries had recently raked in the newspapers. While Jabir took his seat on the table for breakfast, he didn't find Hera. Jabir enquired and was told that Hera was unwell. Jabir paid no heed to Hera's medical condition and continued with his chores. Within fifteen minutes the cavalcade of three vehicles exited the gate and brazenly, siren blaring, went on the road. As if on cue, the few visitors in the tea stall and the barber shop stood with folded hands before the passing cavalcade.

Although Hera was under strict instructions not to use the phone to call any other number except Jabir, Hera picked up the phone and did something she had not done before. She made a missed call to the number mentioned on page 50 of the magazine.

Hera realised she had reached the part of the plan which was at the point of no return. She went outside her room and walked up to the kitchen. Although she usually had no work in the kitchen but sometimes, she did visit the place to kill boredom. Today she went to the kitchen for something else. As she reached the kitchen where two maids were in different stages of preparing meal, she fainted. Her loud thud startled everyone within hearing distance. The maids frantically tried to revive Hera but she was motionless. Someone yelled to call a doctor. The security person called Jabir. The public function where Jabir was the chief guest was already underway when Jabir received a call on his private number. He listened to his security guard and then called his friend who owned the biggest hospital in town. The doctor told Jabir that an ambulance will be at his house within ten minutes. Jabir called back and told the security guard that an ambulance was underway which will take Hera to hospital.

Javed received the missed call and sprang to life. He put on the white coat, took the stethoscope and rushed to the ambulance parked within spitting distance from his room. The daily labourer who was being hired for the last three days without doing any work was fast asleep inside the ambulance. Javed woke him, asked him to sit on the passenger seat and himself took the wheels. Within five minutes of the missed call the ambulance reached Jabir's house. The guards opened the gate without any hesitation. Giving full respect to the doctor, Javed was escorted to the place where Hera was lying motionless. Just behind Javed, the labourer pushed the stretcher. Hera was put on the stretcher and the same was put inside the ambulance. It took just a couple of minutes for Javed to complete the task of taking out Hera from Jabir's house. The ambulance was on its way within a couple of minutes.

While the ambulance with Hera inside had made the first turn towards the next street, it passed another ambulance which was racing towards the street leading to Jabir's house. The second ambulance reached the gate and was halted by the guards. Two doctors alighted from the ambulance and told the guards that they have been sent to take Mrs Jabir to the hospital but the guard looked aghast. He told the doctors that an ambulance had already taken Mrs Jabir to the hospital.

The shrewd mind of Jabir took only a moment to understand what had happened. He had just finished his speech. He told the organizers that due to an urgent work he needed to go. Within fifteen minutes he reached home. Jabir listened to the maids and the security staff about the arrival of two ambulances. He went into his room, opened the almirah and took out his gun. He gestured to his henchmen in the accompanying gypsy van to follow and his car raced out of the gate.

Javed dumped the ambulance approximately two kilometers from Jabir's house. With Hera in tow, he walked briskly looking for a rikshaw to go to Jagdishpur, a hamlet on the outskirts of the town, where his grandparents had a house. After a few denials, Javed finally got a rikshaw. He realised this was the first time he was sitting with Hera. The next part of the plan was to escape recognition from Jabir's henchmen, who as Javed understood, would be in hot pursuit.

While his cavalcade reached city center, Jabir was busy on his phone giving instructions. Within the next ten minutes almost half the city was searching for a young couple who may be travelling in an ambulance. Barely ten minutes later Jabir received a call informing that an abandoned ambulance had been found on a road which goes to Jagdishpur. Jabir's car followed the directions.

Jabir checked the ambulance which had no occupants. He knew Hera and his accomplice would have taken some conveyance from this place. His henchmen started interviewing the passerby and the waiting rikshaw. Finally, somebody told that a young couple was seeking a rikshaw to Jagdishpur. They seemed to be in hurry.

Jabir's car raced forward with the trailing gypsy van on the road to Jagdishpur. Every rikshaw going to Jagdishpur was checked for its occupants. Javed's rikshaw had reached its destination a few minutes earlier. He along with Hera alighted from the rikshaw. Javed realised a lot had changed from the time he last visited this place almost a decade back. He needed to get directions to go to his grandparent house. He saw a tea stall and decided to talk to the people there. Jabir's car reached the Jagdishpur rikshaw stand a few moments later. From behind the tinted glass, Jabir scanned the motley group of people in the open space. His eyes caught the sight of Hera standing alongside a rikshaw. Jabir leapt out of his car, as he advanced towards Hera hurling choiciest expletives, Hera tried to run towards Javed. In that moment, Jabir fired from his gun. Hera had taken only a few strides when the bullet pierced her chest. She fell down.

The sudden turn of events and the gunshot created a commotion in the area. Javed rushed towards Hera. Jabir returned to his car and ordered the driver to return back.

The daylight murder was the talk of the town and the headline in following day newspaper. Amidst public pressure, the police registered an FIR but did not arrest Jabir.

Javed vowed to avenge Hera's murder. Today precisely six years later he was standing in the corner of the sessions court waiting for the Judge to pronounce his judgement in the Hera murder case. The entry of the judge made everybody stand. The judge read the order. Jabir was found guilty of charges under Section 302 of the IPC. The police moved in to arrest Jabir.

With tears in his eyes and a rose in his hand, Javed went to the graveyard and stood beside the grave of Hera. He remembered the girl to whom he could never say 'I want to marry you'.

# 4

## A Tale of Two Generations

The events of this evening continued to haunt Javed. He wanted to sleep but his mind was perplexed, the doctor's observations were indeed depressing. Engrossed in his thoughts, Javed looked at the clock which pronounced that it was 10 minutes past midnight. Silently he turned towards left, Romana was fast asleep. With the AC set at 24° C Romana had the blanket up to her neck. For a few seconds Javed looked at his wife, eight months pregnant she looked beautiful. Javed realised that Romana had gained weight during her pregnancy which gave her a chubby look. He wanted to kiss her but the fear of disturbing her in sleep bore heavily and he curbed his instinct. His right hand slid below the blanket and found Romana's belly bump, he allowed his hand to rest there for a few moments. He felt a movement inside. Javed's mind started conjuring images of the child which was still inside his wife's womb. Romana mumbled something in sleep, Javed retracted his hand and let his wife sleep.

Last evening during the routine checkup, the doctor had told Javed that Romana had high blood pressure which was a cause of worry. In medical terms she was suffering from a condition which was known as Pre-Eclampsia. Prescribing a few medicines, the doctor had cautioned Romana to be careful and advised her to visit the clinic next week.

Javed closed his eyes and tried to sleep. He felt drowsy but his mind felt heavy with the information he had gobbled up from Google about the medical condition categorised as Pre-Eclampsia. In a state of mind somewhere between sleep and conscious thought, Javed's mind took him to the time around six years back when Romana had joined his research lab as a Ph D student. He recollected that Romana was a shy girl giving him lot of respect. She was no different from other students and would always give the impression of doing hard work. Javed's mind was now free from the drowsiness, thinking of Romana when she was his student brought a faint smile on his face. He glanced towards his wife again, the trademark innocence was still there, he realised she was now prettier. Her lips, he observed, had become fuller with time or was it the effect of lipstick which lingered from last evening? He didn't want to tax his mind to find an answer.

Javed opened his eyes and saw the wall clock; both the hands of the clock were superimposed. He sensed it was five minutes past one. Javed tried to sleep but his mind drifted to another pleasant memory somewhere four years before. The Neurochemistry Congress in New Delhi was a prestigious event. Javed had an invited talk and had come to New Delhi with three research students. The assembly elections in Delhi had been announced and the four guests alighting from Prayagraj express found it difficult to get a hotel for stay. After searching for an extended time, they had found a hotel but there were only two rooms available. Javed's mind still had that complex moment frozen in memory. He recollected that it was Romana who had broken the impasse and volunteered that she was willing to share room with Javed Sir.

Javed's memory took him to the awkward moments when he and Romana had entered the hotel room. Romana had behaved in a far more confident manner than him. Although he had left the door slightly open, it was Romana who had bolted the door from inside. This was the first time that Javed was observing Romana so closely. Javed's memories got fixed to the moment when his eyes had met the gaze of Romana while she combed her hair. Even after four years, Javed felt a rush of adrenaline, he recollected that that was the first time he had observed how beautiful Romana looked.

Despite his drill to fall asleep, Javed found himself wide awake when the clock showed thirty minutes past three. The memories of last few years had refreshed his mind. He wanted to recollect more memories but his mind drifted to what the doctor had told him yesterday. A strange sense of abstract fear engulfed him. He didn't realise but sometime later his closed eyes went into sleep mode.

Romana felt a heaviness which was accompanied by palpitation. She glanced towards Javed but found him deep in sleep. She ignored her uneasiness and forced her mind to pleasant thoughts. The palpitation grew stronger, she also felt a bout of nausea. Romana prodded Javed.

It was within half an hour that Romana was wheeled into the operation theatre. A teary-eyed Javed sat on a steel bench praying to the Almighty. The flurry of activity and the urgency of movement in the corridor made Javed more apprehensive. A couple of hours later, Javed saw a grim-faced doctor emerge from the Operation Theatre. Javed took a few steps towards the doctor and his heart sank as he read the look on the face. The doctor told Javed that Romana experienced a massive cardiac arrest while she was being operated for caesarian delivery. Although she could not be saved, the doctors could save the child, a baby boy.

Romana's death changed the course of Javed's fairytale married life. The initial months were extremely challenging. Although Javed's mother and sister took care of the newborn who was given the name Amir, Javed found the going tough without Romana. All the ebullience was replaced with desperation. Javed's smile was now only reserved for moments when Amir played in his lap. At times, while playing with Amir, Javed's eyes would get filled with memories of Romana. Time flew, and Amir was admitted to a preparatory school.

Javed would invariably come home early to catch the evening playing time with Amir. He bought a small cricket bat and taught Amir the basics of batting and bowling. At times when Amir was in playful mood, Javed would get a glimpse of Romana in his countenance.

A good three months had passed while Amir had been attending his school. It was Saturday and the school had given notice of parent-teacher meeting. Javed made it a point to attend the meeting. To his joy, Javed found that the teacher was full of praise for his son. In the evening Javed took Amir to a park and then had dinner in a restaurant.

Sunday morning was lazy. With no pressing engagements Javed slept late. Amir had got up early and was fidgeting with his plastic blocks making building models. It was sometime later at around nine that Amir slipped alongside Javed on the bed and curled himself with hands around his father. Javed was lazily enjoying this show of affection. With his mouth near his father's ears, Amir spoke in a loving voice "papa where is my mummy, all my classmates have mothers but I don't have one". Amir was fortunate that he did not see his father's eyes. Javed felt a lump in his throat, his eyes became wet and he felt that time stood still. Without speaking a word, he turned around and hugged Amir. He continued to hold Amir in embrace till his tear laden eyes had found their natural glint. Amir didn't understand what this gesture conveyed but a basic instinct told him that his father was not comfortable with this question.

Amir was now studying in class five. He mimicked his father in academic pursuits. Both spent long hours at night engrossed in studies. At times, Javed would coax Amir to play chess with him. Javed had very efficiently found a way to play the roles of mother and father to Amir. It was a morning, just before going to school, when Amir complained of stomach ache. Javed told Amir to skip the bus and instead decided to take Amir to school himself. As Amir walked inside the school gate, Javed sensed that something was wrong. In hurried steps he walked towards Amir. Before he could reach Amir at the gate, Amir puked. The vomit was all over his shirt and had also soiled the steps leading to the classroom. Javed had just a small handkerchief. Without a moment lost he cleaned Amir and also knelt down to clean the mess on the stairs. For next three days, Javed took leave from the University to look after Amir at home.

Life continued to go in the forward direction without any pause for the father son duo. Both had found ways to complement each other. A few years passed and Amir was looking forward to his first board examinations. Javed had taken leave from the University to be with Amir during the examinations. Amir passed his examination in flying colours. The next two years seemed to pass in a blink. Amir was getting independent and prepared wholeheartedly for his next board examinations. At times Javed watched his son with a nostalgic look wondering what it would have been if Romana was alive.

Finally, the day had arrived when Amir was out bound to Mumbai for taking admission in the prestigious IIT. The extended family had converged to see off Amir. For several days Javed had been contemplating the contours of his life without Amir. He realised these were the most difficult times ever since he had lost Romana. All through these years he had almost forgot his own joys and sorrows while he found innovative ways to nurture Amir. He realised, off late, he was finding it difficult to climb the stairs to the first floor. In an unexplained gesture, he felt an urge which was irresistible, he opened the drawer of the adjoining table and took out the manila envelope. He took out the photograph of Romana. His moisture filled eyes refracted the light and he found himself looking not at the photograph but the image of Romana which his mind displayed for him. The smiling face in the photograph belied the twenty years that had passed while this photo had found a place in the manila envelope.

Javed found himself lonely in the house after Amir had gone to Mumbai. His only moment of joy was when Amir would make a video call every evening. Javed realised Amir looked happy and contented. In the last few weeks Javed had been experiencing intermittent heaviness in his chest. Today he decided to visit a doctor. A series of tests confirmed that Javed had an ailing heart. The doctor advised Javed to be happy and free of worries. In the evening when Amir called, Javed did not disclose any of his ailments.

Joy returned in the household when Amir came back for fifteen days during the end semester break. For days Javed had made elaborate preparations for Amir. With twenty-one summers behind him, Amir had grown into a handsome young man. Despite some reluctance on the part of Amir, Javed insisted that they both sleep on the same double bed. It was on the fifth night that Amir gingerly told his father that he planned to visit Nainital for a few days with his friends. Javed felt a bit sad, he wanted to spend as much time with Amir but lest his son feel bad, he nodded in consent.

Time continued to flow for Javed who spent hours thinking about Amir. Evening episodes when he would just sit on his arm chair and reminisce how he used to play with Amir became more frequent. More often than not, these episodes would always bring a few tears. With time Javed found a way to bide time.

Five years had passed since Amir had left his home for Mumbai. He had informed his father that a multinational company had shortlisted him during the campus placement. Amir had also informed that before he took up the new assignment, he would visit his hometown for a few days. Javed yearned for the moment when Amir would come calling. He realised it was over eighteen months since Amir had come home.

Amir informed his father that he would be coming home for five days and he would be accompanied by a friend. The joy to see Amir after eighteen months was too pleasant for Javed, he didn't pay heed to the visit of a friend. Javed prepped the home with all his resources, he ensured the kitchen had ample supply of *maggi,* realising that Amir loved it. His heart ached for the moment when Amir would come home. Invariably the lingering thought brought tears to his eyes.

Amir reached home to the tight embrace of his father. Javed could not contain his tears. Once released from the loving hug, Amir introduced Samina to his father. As if on cue Samina adjusted her head scarf and bowed her head in the old fashion style of greeting. Javed's mind was too preoccupied with Amir and thus did not register the gestures of Amir's friend.

It was dinner time and Javed did get time to ponder over the relationship between Amir and Samina. His cultural upbringing did not approve that a girl would accompany a boy to another city for a sojourn. Javed realised that Amir and Samina looked close friends, the bonhomie was clearly visible. His cultural instincts, however, failed to understand why Amir was so loud in his show of affection to Samina. Javed's mind thought that he was growing old and was not in sync with the new generation. His mind did not think beyond the angle of an innocent friendship between Amir and Samina.

Life moved on for Javed. His health was fast deteriorating. Accompanying his long-time heart problem, he was having pain in joints specially the knees. He started living in the past, his only companions being the memories of Romana and Amir's childhood. It was Sunday morning and for a change Javed felt less pain in his knees. He decided to open the big trunk to take out some winter clothing. Digging into the contents he found several things which ignited past memories. There were Romana's dresses and Amir's school uniforms. Javed recognised the first school uniform which Amir had worn when he was admitted to the school. Picking up the dress, a kaleidoscope of memories went past his wet eyes. He decided to keep that dress.

Over the years, the phone calls from Amir to his father had become erratic. The everyday evening video rendezvous call was no more the norm. Since last night Javed was pensive, Amir had informed him that he had decided to marry Samina and that the marriage was fixed for November ten, approximately two weeks from now. Javed was too perplexed to seek any more details. On numerous occasions, when he sat in his armchair, in vacant moods, he had conjured the occasion when he would organize the marriage of Amir. The phone call last night was in fact the last thing he expected.

Given his failing health, Javed did not want to create an unsavory situation lest Amir's happiness be compromised. He felt that his only means of happiness was Amir. Javed booked the air ticket to Pune for a date two days before the marriage and informed Amir that he was coming for the marriage function.

Amir received Javed at the airport, he hugged his father. The overdose of oxytocin that Javed's brain produced when Amir hugged him melted his heart. He forgot all those questions pertaining to Samina and the marriage which he had thought during the flight. Javed's mind thought of Romana. Nostalgia overtook his thoughts, he reminisced how Amir would embrace him during school days when he would return home.

Javed observed that the marriage function was only a reception. The traditional rituals involving a groom and bride were nowhere to be seen. Both Amir and Samina were welcoming guests' hand-in-hand. To Javed's perception, in that violet midriff baring ensemble, Samina looked embarrassingly exposed. Javed sat in a corner; nobody paid any heed to the old man sitting at the far end of the hall. Javed silently observed the changing face of new generation, he realised that he was totally out of place in those disco lights, liquor gulping crowd and exotic menu. Nobody took notice when after a couple of hours, the old man took a cab and returned home.

According to Javed's booking he had to take the return flight a couple of days post marriage ceremony. However, disaster struck the next day after the reception. It was already eleven in the morning but no one had cared to serve Javed a cup of tea. Javed decided to help himself trying to make tea in the kitchen. Although he had made tea every day in his home but he found the new gadgets difficult to handle. Making extra effort not to make a noise, he spilled the hot water onto his hands. An involuntary shriek filled the small flat. Amir came running and found his father in intense pain. A couple of hours later, with a heavily bandaged left hand, Javed lay on his bed cursing why he decided to make tea himself.

With flight ticket cancelled, Javed was left with no choice but to stay with Amir. The small flat, at times, provided little privacy. On numerous occasions Javed felt awkward when Samina would pass his sight in those skimpy dresses. On several occasions Javed had to interact with Samina, he observed that of late her gait was different. It was after a series of observations that Javed's mind understood what was wrong with Samina. He realised that Samina was pregnant. Javed felt too embarrassed to confirm this observation with Amir.

Time passed. Javed had no option but to remain confined in his room. With diverse ailments already in his kitty, the wound on his left hand made him almost an invalid. Samina was now heavily pregnant, it was Amir who tended to the exigencies of both Samina and his father.

It was late Friday night when Javed heard some loud conversation from the adjoining bedroom. He could make out the shrill feminine voice of Samina. Some of the words were audible. Despite being short of hearing, Javed could make out the essence of the harsh communication. He understood that the conversation wobbled around his continued presence in the house.

Night was difficult to pass, Javed felt heavy at heart not only on his plight but also what Amir must be undergoing. He waited for the morning. When Amir came to his room at nine with a cup of tea, Javed asked him to spend a few moments with him. Amir was in a hurry and asked him to tell him the reason. In a choking voice Javed told Amir that he had decided to move to an old age home in Pune. No words were spoken. Amir left the room.

Javed again heard the same set of conversation between Amir and Samina this afternoon. He could make out that this time also it was to do something with his stay in the house. It was at around four in the evening that Javed called a taxi. Amir fleetingly protested to his father not to leave them but it was apparent that he too was under tremendous mental strain.

The next day, Amir visited his father at the Old Age Home. He was ushered in a dim lit room which had four occupants. On the far side, Javed was lying on a cot, there was just a single chair in the room, probably this place had few visitors. Amir spent sometime with his father giving him the apples which he had purchased while coming.

Amir returned home with mixed emotions. He felt let down by the fact that Samina did not show any remorse at the sad decision of father opting to stay at Old Age home. The weekend passed without any further discord. Amir prepared dinner and did the chores. Samina's lazy demeanor blatantly portrayed that she was almost full time. The next few weeks passed slowly. Amir and Samina looked expectantly forward to each passing day.

It started just after midnight on Friday night. Samina started experiencing contractions and the doctor admitted her. The previous ultrasound had revealed that there was some problem with placenta and that her delivery may be complicated. While Samina was taken to the ICU, Amir waited outside praying to Almighty. A couple of hours passed without any word from inside. It was after a painstaking three hours that the doctor asked Amir to meet her in the chamber. The look on the face of the doctor was tense. She informed Amir that the pregnancy was very difficult and in the process of

C-section, Samina delivered a stillborn baby. However, the good news was that they could save her wife.

Amir was distraught. He met Samina in the ICU. The pain of losing her child was oozing from her countenance. As per religious customs, Amir prepared the body of the baby and silently carried him to the graveyard in his lap.

The Noorani Masjid Cemetry had evolved a mechanism to keep track of graves for times to come. Upon a request for a funeral the office would take the required grave digging fee and allot a number. The relatives carrying the dead would then have to visit the cemetery where the grave would be ready and marked with the identification number. Amir was allotted number 265 for the grave of his son.

When Amir arrived at the cemetery, he found the spot where grave number 265 was ready but had to wait as some people were still in the process of burying their dead in the adjoining grave which bore the number 264. It took another twenty minutes for Amir to complete the formalities and return to the hospital to take care of Samina.

A week had passed since Samina lost the child. Life was limping back with Amir. It was Friday morning and he realised that he had not visited his father for the last ten days. Samina's condition had been critical for the last one week and he had not got time to visit the Old Age home.

Amir reached the Old Age home and enroute entered the office where he expected to find the old lady who would take him inside. The lady was there but she gave Amir a puzzling look. Sensing that Amir missed her stare, she told Amir that it's been a week since Javed, his father, had died. Glancing through the register she continued that he died on last Friday and as per his wishes his last rites were performed at the Noorani Masjid Cemetry where his grave number was 264. The lady informed Amir that Javed had categorically mentioned in writing that upon his death, if it happened within this month, his son should not be informed.

Amir felt lost. He realised that even in death Papa did not want to burden him. Till Amir remained lost in his thoughts, the lady at the counter handed him a bundle which she said were the remains his father had left. Teary eyed, with a thousand thoughts of his late father brewing in his mind, Amir opened the bundle. On the top was a neatly folded school dress. Amir remembered the day when as a toddler his father had taken him to school and he had followed him catching hold of his forefinger.

# 5

# When Belief Came Crumbling

The child convulsed. Taskera held him close to her bosom, she could feel the rising temperature of the child's body. Her sunken white eyes were bereft of emotion. She tilted her head to peep outside the window and realised it was still an hour to sunset. Holding the child closer to her bosom, she pulled the blouse upwards allowing the child access to her sagging nipples. The child had little strength even to suckle, she continued to hold her young child in her lap. Her creased face showed no reaction. In the other corner of the thatched cottage, Jamrul sat, knees bent, smoking a bidi.

Jagdishpur, a tiny hamlet on the banks of river Tons was a sleepy village with a native population that had always considered modern technology an anathema. Traditional customs and beliefs, some several centuries old, provided an unsaid glue to the society which by choice was averse to modern technology. Life followed an altogether different pace in Jagdishpur, much like the flow in the river Tons which was so slow that it hardly seemed to move.

The two graves, sitting on a crumbling pedestal on the bank of the river, occupied a revered place in the hierarchy of beliefs among the natives of Jagdishpur. Nobody knew the historical truth of these structures but the folklore ascribed great powers to be associated with the gentlemen who, as natives believed, occupied their hallowed place inside the graves.

Come Thursday and the area around the graves would become a mini bazaar. Sweetmeat shops selling fake saffron coloured *laddoos* and fluffy sugar cakes sprang up from nowhere. Women spread their hand made bamboo crafts on old muslin cloth spread on the parched mud. Men carrying makeshift bamboo stands sold red and yellow ribbons and scarves. The mini bazaar would come to life just after sunset when the caretakers of the graves, in green sequined attire, took their place beside the two crumbling structures decorated heavily with flowers and incense sticks.

Visitors in different hues would converge from far away villages. They all paid obeisance to the graves with silent prayers in their hearts. The caretakers deftly collected money from the visitors without any obvious effort. Among the visitors to the graves were old, infirm and sick seeking good health, mothers carrying ill and malnourished children praying for the wellbeing, able bodied males praying silently for sustenance. There were also families which came for getting divine help to ward off evil spirits. Young women were brought for evicting demons, djinns, or other spiritual entities.

Today was a Thursday and Taskera looked forward to taking her two-year-old child to the village's revered spot to seek the blessing of the two dead men in an effort to cure her child's illness. Clutching the child close to her chest she made way through the beaten path across the meadow to the bank of the river Tons. Since her childhood Taskera had seen her grandparents and parents follow this ritual for seeking divine help to cure diseases, solve family disputes and provide relief from the evil effects of ghosts and evil spirits.

The spot adjoining the graves was bustling with activity when Taskera reached the place just after sunset. She made her way through the group of women who had come to this place to be cured through exorcism. The custodian of the graves was busy mumbling some inaudible verses and handing over a part of the offering of sweetmeat pieces. In his left hand he held an assortment of crumbled currency notes which had been given by visitors as part of their fee for seeking the divine intervention.

When her turn came, Taskera held the child on her hands in an extended position and looked towards the custodian of the graves. The man with a mystical appearance and a long beard looked at the child and waved a peacock feather over the face of the child. He sprinkled a few drops of holy water on the face and the lips of the semi-comatose child. The sudden sensation of cold water made the child stir. Taskera found a ten rupee note which she had concealed inside her blouse, she silently pushed the note in the left hand of the man in the green sequined dress and took a few steps back without turning backwards. This was a ritual which everyone followed in an effort to show respect to the divine powers of the occupants of the grave. As she moved back someone else moved forward. The routine continued. Taskera took the return journey along the same path with relief in her mind. She felt the child's body was less hot. Silently she thanked the divine power of the grave.

While Taskera was away seeking divine help through obeisance to the graves, Jamrul found time to go to his friend Sabir's cottage a few lanes away. Jamrul knew Sabir would not be at home, he usually went to pick rags after evening.

Jamrul found Sabir's wife Chenu at the door. Chenu was the heart-throb of the locality. Although not very fair but her charming looks and soft voice was a magnet for the menfolk. Jamrul also had a soft corner for Chenu. Often, he gifted her with artificial jewellry and makeup kits. Today also he carried a silver-coloured anklet for Chenu. There had been some instances in the past when Chenu had allowed Jamrul to satisfy his instincts. Jamrul implored Chenu for a fling, she said a passive 'no'. Jamrul perceived her 'no' as a 'yes'. He pulled her towards him. There was a sound of rikshaw outside, Chenu realised Sabir had come home. She pulled herself away from Jamrul.

When Taskera returned home she did not find Jamrul. She checked the few aluminum containers and found them to be empty save for a few fistfuls of rice in one of them. Today she had no money, the money she had, had been spent on her visit to the grave. The child was restless. Taskera felt his forehead, she realised it was hot. She glanced around the cottage. Her eldest daughter and two younger sons had gone to sleep without dinner. A drop of tear was still fresh in the eyes of the young son who was just a year older than the one in Taskera's lap. Taskera emptied all the rice in a utensil and put it on flame.

Jamrul's wishes remained unfulfilled this evening. As he returned from Chenu's shanty, his strides meandered towards the liquor shop. He had a ten rupee note in his pocket. He put his hand across the grill and pulled it back with a pouch. He reached home with his mind now relieved of all problems. The intoxicated mind also did not register the plight of three hungry children sleeping on the floor. With senses beyond his control, Jamrul using a few expletives asked Taskera to give something to eat. Taskera put the full pot of boiled rice before her husband. Seeing the bland rice infuriated Jamrul, in rage he kicked the pot. The rice spilled on the floor.

Taskera lay on the floor with the ailing child. With scant sense of belonging, Jamrul lay on the only cot in the cottage. Taskera put a hand on the forehead of her son. She felt the heat, there was also a wheezing sound while the child breathed. She lay motionless and lost count of her thoughts when her eyes closed. It was around four in the morning when, to an unknown mother's instinct, Taskera woke and touched the forehead of her child. She felt the cold skin. She felt a strange sensation. The child was motionless and very still. A shriek came out from Taskera's dry mouth. She grabbed the limp body and hugged it tightly. The body remained limp and cold. Somewhere far in the locality a *muezzin* was saying the *azaan* calling the faithful to the prayers. Word spread fast. Some women from the neighbourhood trooped in. Someone sent a polythene bag containing tea and a pack of biscuits. Today, while the youngest of them lay dead a few feet away, the three hungry children got an early tea with a handful of biscuits.

Grief was always ephemeral in this society. There were so many challenges in everyday life that grieving over the loss of a child was a luxury. The next morning came with fresh needs of lunch and dinner. Taskera had to reach the place where she worked as a domestic help and therefore, she left home early. Jamrul loitered in the lanes doing nothing. For the last many years Jamrul had lived with the notion that he was under the influence of an evil spirit which didn't allow him to work. He had visited the sacred graves many a times and even the custodian with the long beard had used his divine powers to help Jamrul. The society and especially Taskera easily bought his argument without protest. It was, therefore, on this pretext that Jamrul had become dependent on Taskera for earning a living.

Life moved on in Jagdishpur. The Thursdays, as usual, brought the village folk to the sacred graves for divine help in matters as diverse as disease, employment, matrimony and escape from evil spirit. In the last few years, the village bazaar had seen many qualified doctors open clinics but the belief in the divine powers of the graves had made very few villagers to go to doctors for cure.

While Jagdishpur was moving at a snail's pace, something exciting was happening in New Delhi. Following the American initiative of creating many smart cities in India, the French foreign minister had showed interest in adopting a few villages, preferably the most backward, and creating infrastructure matching international standards. An MoU had been signed between the Indian and the French governments in this regard.

The Ambassador of France to India Marie Clemente had been posted in New Delhi for just over a couple of months. She had not been able to see India. When she received the responsibility of identifying five villages for development as part of the 'smart village' initiative she realised it was a difficult task. She decided to take a tour of two of the most populous states, Uttar Pradesh and Bihar.

Criss-crossing the difficult terrain sometimes on helicopter, at times by road and mostly by foot, Marie Clemente prepared detailed notes. After an arduous exploration of the villages of Uttar Pradesh and Bihar for seventeen days, she submitted her report and the names of the designated villages to Government of India. In the list submitted by the Ambassador, Jagdishpur was also present.

Work started in earnest for the ambitious French Government project. A team of engineers, environmentalists and planners visited Jagdishpur. News had percolated within the general populace that large scale changes were going to be made in the village. Rather than feeling happy, most of the inhabitants were skeptical. The issue had also found an echo in the village panchayat. The general consensus favoured some kind of a protest against the proposal.

Within six months of the MoU being inked between the two Governments, the proposal was approved. According to the master plan the landscape of Jagdishpur would be changed drastically. Among the initiatives to be implemented included a multispecialty hospital, a primary and secondary school, an area devoted to small industries and a vocational training center. To create employment opportunities, the master plan proposed development of the scenic riverbank of Tons into an amusement park.

Within a couple of months, just after the monsoon, the cranes and bulldozers started arriving at Jagdishpur. Village men and women witnessed the activities with displeasure. The work started in earnest under the supervision of French engineers. Bulldozers started levelling the ground. With security in place no one dared to question the supervisors who gave orders for the work. It was a Friday morning when the bulldozers rased the two dilapidated graves and the pedestal on which they stood. Within a day the whole landscape of the river bank had changed. The villagers looked aghast; the divine powers of the graves had vanished in dust.

Taskera too was in the crowd which witnessed the razing of the graves. Resonating the silent prayers of many in the crowd, Taskera also believed that some supernatural power would stop the bulldozers from levelling the graves. Nothing happened. Among the crowd of onlookers also stood the caretaker of the two graves who, despite being a tailor by profession, made money on every Thursday selling false hopes to a gullible innocent population.

Today Jagdishpur is a 'smart village'. The services at the hospital ensure that no lives are lost due to want of medical attention. A few months back, Jamrul had also started to ply a rikshaw, convinced that there are no evil spirits.

# 6

# Why Did You Marry Me?

The lecture hall of the Motilal Nehru Medical College was brimming with bright young faces, all radiating a common glow of intelligence. Despite the crowd there were very few murmurs of conversation. It was the first Monday of September when the new medical students had assembled for their first lecture in the Medical College. The lecture hall built in the theatre style looked large for this group of fifty students. The unfamiliarity amongst the group was evident by the fact that the girls were huddled in the first two rows. The remaining boys were sprinkled sparsely in the upper rows.

Sitting in the left corner of the third row, Asif looked aimlessly waiting for the Professor to arrive. His mind drifted to the memory of long hours he had spent preparing for the NEET examination. He realised this was the moment of truth for which he and his parents had always dreamt. His memory drifted to the trauma when his father had taken a loan from the provident fund to pay for his exorbitant coaching fee. A thin tear covered his eyes when he recollected the look on the faces of his parents after he had broken the news of his qualification in the NEET examination. Asif's floating thoughts abruptly ended when he saw the Professor walk into the class.

Nothing much happened in the class. The Professor started by asking everyone to introduce themselves. The sequence started from the front row with girls introducing themselves. As each girl stood and spoke a few introductory sentences, Asif's mind started practicing what he was expected to say when his turn came. It was a few seconds later when the introductions reached the second row that Asif heard a girl introduce herself as Zeba from St Mary's Convent, Allahabad. By the time he could see the girl properly, it was the turn of the next student to introduce. A few seconds later it was Asif's turn and he introduced himself. As the introductions moved to other students, Asif's eyes meandered towards Zeba. She was seated in the right corner and Asif had just a side view. Before he could see her properly, the Professor started speaking and Asif got engrossed into the lecture.

That night while he was reminiscing the events of his first day at the medical college, Asif couldn't escape the thought of Zeba. There was something in that girl which was infectious. Asif focused his thoughts on revising the first lecture, he opened the book on his table, Lehninger's Biochemistry.

The girl's hostel was just a few hundred yards from the boy's hostel. It was Zeba's first night in the hostel. Returning from the class, she had taken a short nap. Still in bed and using the pillow as a cushion, she picked her Biochemistry book and absentmindedly flipped through the pages. Her mind, still not agreeing to read the book, drifted to the memory of the class in the morning. Her mind stumbled upon the sight of the lanky boy, sitting on the other side in the third row, who had introduced himself as Asif. Her mind coaxed her to align the tone of the boy to a far memory which was so hazy that it was impossible to recollect. She tried hard to recollect. With eyes aimlessly fixed on a distant wall, she found a probable answer some minutes later. A faint memory of a four-year-old boy in school uniform who used to share the same rikshaw trolley while she, as a small girl in blue tunic and skirt of Saint Mary's school, took that same conveyance, became visible. Zeba's face lit up with a smile. She remembered that the boy's name was Asif. Without any obvious intention, Zeba closed the book and her eyelids drooped. *She went back in time. She was a small girl and was going to school on a rikshaw trolley with ten other small children. Asif was seated just a few feet away on the other seat.*

Zeba saw Asif in the corridor the next morning. Her eyes started finding resemblance between her present classmate and the boy who used to share the same rikshaw some eighteen years back. Asif walked past Zeba oblivious of what was going on in the mind of the beautiful girl who had introduced herself as Zeba in the introductions yesterday.

A week had passed and groups had started to emerge among classmates. The girls mostly kept within themselves. On numerous occasions Zeba found it interesting to observe Asif while he conversed with other boys. She realised that Asif's mannerisms were almost the same that he used to display some eighteen years back. At times Zeba did get a feeling that Asif was observing her but Asif always looked blank when at times he met her gaze.

It was around the eighth week that practical classes started and students were divided in groups. Zeba found it interesting to see that Asif was in the same group as she was. A few days had passed while Zeba tried to strike a conversation with Asif. It was on the third day during one practical class, while the group was waiting for the spectrophotometer to be free from the earlier group, that Zeba popped the question to Asif asking him whether he is the same Asif who went to Boys High School in a rikshaw trolley from the Chowk locality almost eighteen years back. Asif felt bemused. His mind catapulted him to the time when he was in class one and went to school on a rikshaw trolley along with ten other children. While a smiling Zeba observed Asif's reaction, Asif's brain took very little time to bring back the image of a chubby girl in blue uniform who used to fight with him for the corner seat inside the trolley. Asif's countenance said it all. His eyes looked straight at Zeba's line of sight. They both smiled.

A couple of months had passed and several friendships were blossoming. The groups had become defined and conversation had changed from pleasantries to personal. Asif looked forward to moments when he and Zeba would visit the canteen for coffee breaks. Time passed. Friends too became used to the sight of Asif and Zeba sharing candid moments.

December was cold and the first semester examinations had been announced. Most students studied past midnight preparing for the examinations. It had become a routine that Asif would call Zeba and would meet her in the front garden after dinner. Both would take a lazy stroll for ten minutes and then go to their hostels. The rules of the hostel prohibited members of the other sex visiting each other's hostel. That chilly night Zeba clung closer to Asif. Asif felt the warmth of her body. Their hands explored the unexplored. For a moment time stood still. Zeba stood on her toes to reach Asif's face. She kissed him.

The next five years saw Asif and Zeba live life in romance. Examinations came and went. Finally, the time came when the medical course came to an end. All students were making hectic preparations for the post graduate NEET examination.

When the results came Asif did very well to get Oncology and Zeba was admitted to Pediatrics. The subjects were different and so was the departments and the time table. For days Asif found it difficult to get time to sneak a visit to Pediatrics department.

Initially Zeba felt a void but as time passed, she became accustomed to her new routine. The new hostel for girls was far from PG Boys Hostel and the routine of after dinner strolls also ended. Time is a big healer and the pangs of growing distance with Asif became subdued. Zeba started to find new friends with whom she spent time. Asif remained in her loop with almost daily telephone calls.

The Pediatrics department was going to celebrate its centenary celebration and an elaborate function had been planned. Among the academic programmes there was a cultural event to be followed by dinner. The post graduate students were given the responsibility of the cultural event. Zeba was a livewire and was coordinating the events. The rehearsals usually took place in the evenings after the classes got over. Sidharth was taking part in several programmes. He was a talented singer and also played drums.

The heavy workload of studies never allowed the luxury of personal interactions on normal days but the preparations of the cultural event brought the students closer. Zeba had many interactions with Sidharth and she found him to be a highly intelligent boy. As days passed, Zeba could just not ignore her silent admiration for Sidharth. At times, she realised, she would listen to his songs with an intent that was beyond normal admiration.

The glittering cultural night started with the opening speech by Zeba. In that dark maroon thigh-slit evening gown she looked ethereal. Other events followed but Sidharth stole the lime light. The crowd continued to ask for more while he finished his quota of songs. The eloquent admiration of the crowd also had an echo in Zeba's heart. As Sidharth finished his performance, backstage Zeba could not restrain herself and she hugged Sidharth. In that spontaneous show of emotion by Zeba, Sidharth felt a joy which was alien to him.

The function finished and whether it was a coincidence or providence, Sidharth found himself seated next to Zeba. Zeba radiated glow and Sidharth played the role of a perfect gentleman. Post dinner, Sidharth offered Zeba to drop her to her hostel. That night, Zeba forgot to call Asif. Almost half a kilometer away in the PG Boy's hostel, Sidharth realised he was thinking more of Zeba than his stupendous singing performance.

The next day Zeba found she was trying to locate Sidharth in the class. Always a bit shy, today even Sidharth looked up to Zeba and waived. Life had taken a new turn for Zeba. After the class Zeba found she was waiting for Sidharth to break free of his friends and come to her. Absentmindedly they walked without reason to the coffee shop. While Zeba was having coffee her phone rang. She glanced at the screen and silently ignored the call. On the other end of the line Asif found it strange. His last three calls had gone unanswered.

A few months passed with Zeba living an intoxicated beautiful life in the company of Sidharth. During evenings, Sidharth would sing old songs which Zeba liked. It was again a cold December night when Zeba received a call from Sidharth post-midnight. Groggy eyed Zeba answered the call, an excited Sidharth informed her that he had got a fellowship to pursue post graduate studies at the Internal Medicine Department of Pisa University. Sidharth informed her that the fellowship starts from next month and that he intended to go to Italy. A pause followed before Sidharth found courage to say that he loved her and wanted her to come along. Zeba's mind went into a spin. A kaleidoscope of thoughts engulfed her brain. Despite her desire to be in the company of Sidharth, the whole idea of moving to Italy was fraught with many uncertainties.

Events happened fast after that late night development. Zeba convinced her parents that she would be happy with Sidharth and would also find some medical course to pursue in Italy. Paperwork and visa were arranged. Within few weeks, Zeba and Sidharth were boarding the Alitalia flight for Rome enroute to the Leaning tower city of Pisa.

The departure of Sidharth and Zeba in the middle of the PG course was a perfect food for gossip within the Medical College social media. Asif too heard this news. For several months he had very little contact with Zeba but the stark reality still hurt him. He felt sad and forlorn.

With Zeba no long a factor in Asif's life, Asif had very few distractions. He put all his energy in the PG Oncology course. Even before the scheduled completion of his course, Asif had several employment offers from leading hospitals. Within a week after getting his M.D. Degree, Asif joined the Regency Hospital in Kanpur as Chief Oncologist.

Asif took up his new responsibility with elan. He felt fortunate to find a decent rent accommodation in the nearby Sarvodaya Nagar within half a kilometer from Regency Hospital. Mrs Ghosh, the landlady, was a petite woman probably in her fifties. She had recently lost her husband due to COVID and lived alone with a daughter, Sunaina, who was pursuing her Ph D in English.

The hectic workload in the hospital was energy sapping and Asif was always longing for leisure time when he would indulge in his once favourite pastime of writing short stories. On rare occasions when Asif got a day off, he found it interesting to browse the collection of books in the bookshelves of Mrs Ghosh's apartment. There were full collections of Larry Collins & Dominique Lappierre, Leon Uris, Fredrick Forsyth, and Mario Puzo. Another shelf stalked classics which included Lewis Carroll's Alice in Wonderland, Homer's Odyssey, Jane Austen's Pride and Prejudice among others. Asif found it mouthwatering when his eyes fell upon the book of short stories by O'Henry. He wanted to ask Mrs Ghosh to take the book for reading but resisted the urge.

With only three people in the apartment, it was but natural that Sunaina did bump into Asif usually during mornings or late evenings. During these brief interactions Sunaina found the Doctor a perfectly mannered young man. However, in all the interactions there were only brief exchange of pleasantries. On one of the days, Sunaina did observe that Asif had paused to browse the bookshelf and was taking interest in the books on display. She felt amused, after all Oncology and Literature were poles apart.

A couple of months had passed since Asif had joined Regency hospital. Mrs Ghosh was happy with her new tenant. In Asif she discovered a perfect human, he was never late in paying his rent and lived a frugal lifestyle barely showing any signs of extravagance. Candidly, Mrs Ghosh sometimes thought that if she had a son, he would have been like Asif. In the last three months, she had not seen any indications of ill manners or any addiction in Asif.

It was the month of Ramazan and Mrs Ghosh realised that Asif was observing fast. She heard him wake up in the last quarter of night and prepare something in the kitchen. The next day Mrs Ghosh set an alarm and woke in the wee hours and visit the kitchen. She found Asif preparing tea for himself. Mrs Ghosh asked Asif to sit while she prepared a healthy meal for Asif. In the morning, while Asif had already gone to the hospital, Mrs Ghosh asked Sunaina to bring a packet of dates when she returned from the University.

It was a December afternoon and being a Sunday, Asif also had an off day. In the last six months, the initial reluctance of talking to Sunaina had waned. Today while he was browsing the books on the shelf, Asif found Sunaina watching him. Taking the book of short stories by O'Henry, Asif walked up to Sunaina and asked her whether he can borrow the book to read. Sunaina looked startled, she could never imagine that someone who cured cancer patients and had an outward appearance of a serious person would be having such a literary taste. With a gleeful countenance she said 'yes'. The ice being broken between the two, Sunaina asked Asif whether he had read O'Henry before, Asif's face lit up, without taking a moment he said that he had read O'Henry's 'The Last Leaf' and 'The Gift of the Magi'. What started like a benign interlude, continued for over an hour. Both Asif and Sunaina talked about literature. Sunaina found out that Asif was very well read. They talked about Charles Dickens, Ernest Hemingway and Paulo Coelho. After his failed romance with Zeba, this was the first time Asif had talked in a relaxed manner with a girl. Despite being living in this house for the last six months, Asif had never given any thought to Sunaina's looks. Today while he engaged her in conversation, he realised she was enticingly beautiful.

As Asif returned to his room, clutching the book of short stories, he found he was humming an old Bollywood number. He felt happy.

The next Sunday it was again an off day for Asif. Not because he had completed reading the book, Asif searched for Sunaina to return the book. For an unknown reason Asif's mind was coaxing him to continue the conversation that started last week. Sunaina too felt happy to see Asif. The conversation again continued for an hour. Sunaina offered to make a cup of coffee and Asif did not object.

The conversation between Sunaina and Asif which till now was confined to books and literature, drifted to more worldly affairs. Both realised they had many common interests. Asif felt delighted when Sunaina told him that she considered Maradona a better player than Pele. Sunaina started looking forward to evenings when Asif would return from hospital early.

On the next Monday, due to an emergency, Asif had to go to the hospital early in the morning. When he came back that afternoon, there was a piece of paper sticking on his door. Asif read the paper. In bold handwriting a message was scribbled *"Today is my birthday, please come home early. We will celebrate and also have dinner together, Sunaina".*

It had been almost four years when Asif had last walked into a store to buy something feminine. Today as he walked into the *HM* store in Kanpur's Z Square Mall, there was some excitement in his stride. His eyes scanned the gleaming dresses on display. Today every mannequin looked like Sunaina. He chose a bright red ensemble without looking at the price. On his way back to home, he stopped at the florist and asked for a Biedermeier bouquet. The florist asked him whether he needed a card. Asif paused; his mind debated many options. He realised his mind was not agreeing with what his heart wanted. Today he let his heart do the talking. He chose the card with the tagline "***to my love***". He signed the card and placed it inside the bouquet.

Sunaina looked resplendent in her birthday dress. With only two people in attendance, she cut the cake. Asif sang a few muted lines of *Happy Birthday to you.....* Sunaina put a piece of cake in her mother's mouth and then in a display of emotional freedom made Asif eat the cake from her hands. Asif reciprocated and made her eat the remaining piece from his hands. Mrs Ghosh, with a glint of tears of joy, watched her daughter get cozy with Asif.

Asif felt an excitement in life which he had lost for so many years. Almost every day, Sunaina would wait till Asif returned from the hospital. They both had dinner together.

It was a Monday night when Asif didn't find Sunaina at the dining table. He softly knocked at Mrs Ghosh's room. Once he heard Mrs Ghosh asking him to come inside, Asif asked why Sunaina had slept early. Mrs Ghosh informed Asif that Sunaina was not feeling well and she wanted to take rest.

Things returned to normal the next day but Asif found Sunaina a bit run down although Sunaina reiterated that she was well. It was a few days later that Sunaina again felt weak and also complained of nausea. This time she told Asif about her status and Asif gave her a few medicines. Things became normal.

Diwali was round the corner and festivities were being planned in Ghosh household. On the Diwali night when Mrs Ghosh, Sunaina and Asif sat for dinner, Mrs Ghosh started in a tone which was in effect addressed to both Sunaina and Asif. After short introductory words, Mrs Ghosh came to the point. She extolled the virtues of marriage and said that it the fitness of things she would be happy if Asif and Sunaina get married. Asif felt a sigh of relief, he wanted to say the same thing to Sunaina for a long time but could not find the right moment. Sunaina was lost in thought; it was in this moment that her eyes caught the sight of the small pink card inside the bouquet which Asif had brought. Her moist eyes read the words "***to my love***". She blushed. She turned towards Asif. Asif extended his hand towards Sunaina and she held it. A few tears came down from Mrs Ghosh's eyes.

Life had a new meaning for both Sunaina and Asif post that Diwali night. The Ghosh household was continuously bathed in joy. Mrs Ghosh loved the subtle show of affection which she sometimes witnessed between Sunaina and Asif. Asif told his parents and got their consent. He also informed the hospital that he would be taking two weeks leave. Once granted he told Sunaina. It was again at dinner time that the date of the marriage was fixed.

Asif realised that Sunaina had lost some weight in recent weeks. While science can boost to have solved the mysteries of the universe, it is still difficult to decipher a woman's mind. Asif thought, with marriage round the corner, Sunaina must be dieting. Some days passed when Sunaina again complained of weakness and nausea. Asif found that she looked pale. Asif's mind contemplated several options. His mind tried to escape any serious illness. However, not taking any chances, Asif asked Sunaina to visit the hospital and give a blood sample for pathology tests.

His mind raced to find an answer. The blood parameters of Sunaina were loud and clear. Sunaina was in the second stage of blood cancer. Today as Asif went through the pathology report, he wished that everything which was written there was wrong. In the past, on hundreds of occasions, he had told his patients that pathological tests are done by computers and cannot be wrong, but today he wished otherwise. For a change today Asif was not a doctor but a guardian.

Sunaina was waiting when Asif returned home. Asif hugged Sunaina and presented her with a rose which he had picked from the florist on his way back. Sunaina insisted to know what was in her blood report. Asif reassured her that everything was fine and she will be fine. To divert her thoughts, Asif discussed at length the preparations of her marriage. After dinner, Asif gave her some medicines which were not the usual ones which Sunaina was taking. Sunaina looked perplexed but didn't say anything.

Sunaina continued to lose weight. Her bouts of nausea became more frequent and she felt weak. Asif conducted more tests and coaxed her to take more medicines. Sunaina found it difficult to understand what was happening but remained clueless. Asif kept on encouraging her. Almost every day he would come home early from the hospital and his show of affection became more pronounced.

Just a few days were left for the marriage. Sunaina was fighting a losing battle. She was forcing her body to find the energy to live up to others' expectations. Friends and relatives were enjoying the festivities. Sunaina laboured hard to put out a brave face.

Marriage was solemnised. Finally, Asif and Sunaina became Husband and Wife. Mrs Ghosh was extremely happy. While Sunaina and Asif had been busy in marriage preparations, Mrs Ghosh had been visiting an attorney to create a will. Today, as Asif and Sunaina returned home, she presented them with inheritance papers for all the properties which were hitherto in Mrs Ghosh's name.

It was in the morning that Asif informed Sunaina that they would be going to Mumbai for honeymoon. Today Sunaina was feeling much worse but she forced a smile. The flight from Kanpur to Mumbai took two hours. As Asif walked towards the exit, he located the waiting ambulance. Before booking the flight he had already booked an appointment at the Tata Memorial Cancer Hospital. Sunaina looked aghast at the turn of events. Within two hours of landing at Mumbai airport, she was admitted in the Tata Memorial Cancer Hospital.

After a detailed examination and over a dozen tests which took two days, the doctors informed Asif that Sunaina's cancer had already gone past the stage of remission. At best she had only one weeks' time. This afternoon when Asif entered Sunaina's room, he could not control his tears. He looked aged. The hospital environment and the flurry of doctors had already made Sunaina understand her condition. A distraught Asif sat beside her. Sunaina took Asif's hand in her hand. She could barely speak. When Asif looked at her, she asked him **'why did you marry me'**.

Asif returned to Kanpur within a week of his going to Mumbai. The loss of Sunaina was too hard for Mrs Ghosh. The house looked desolate. Asif kept himself locked in his room. Of and on someone would drop in on a condolence visit, which was again a painful moment for the grieving Asif and Mrs Ghosh. Life again lost its reason for Asif.

The next six months passed so slowly for Asif that it seemed almost a decade. Asif tried to spend as much time in the hospital as possible. He started his research laboratory in the hospital working on molecular mechanisms leading to oncogenic transformation. It was a Friday when Asif didn't find Mrs Ghosh during the breakfast. He decided to visit her room. Mrs Ghosh was already cold. From his medical training, Asif could understand it was more than 4-5 hours that she was dead. Asif was left alone to live with Sunaina's memories.

Two years had passed since the tragic death of Sunaina. Asif was doing well in research. His latest research paper in the Journal of Clinical Oncology was being considered as a landmark finding. All his energies were focused on research. It was Monday and Asif had come back from laboratory very late. Before sleeping he checked his email. There was an invitation from the World Congress of Medicine inviting Dr Asif to present his findings on cancer in the meeting to be held in Rome, Italy the next month.

The University of Roma Tre at Tor Vergata was quite far from downtown Rome. The conference was being organised in the main hall or The Sala Principale. The opening session saw participants from all parts of the world. There were only a few delegates from India. After the opening session chaired by the Rector of the University of Roma Tre, the session broke for refreshments. Asif roamed the hall but found no one to whom he could talk. Suddenly his eyes found a face which made him stop. Walking towards him was Zeba. A good six years had passed since he last saw her. Time seemed to have had a very little effect on Zeba. She looked almost the same. Asif looked towards Zeba and realised she had already seen him and was purposely walking towards him. Zeba extended her hand and reluctantly Asif shook it. Asif felt a bit awkward but Zeba was more forthcoming. She found a quiet spot in a corner and asked Asif to accompany her there.

After a few ginger moments, things became normal. Asif enquired about Sidharth. Zeba's expression became sad. She informed that within six months after they had come to Italy, Sidharth had died in a road accident. Asif became emotional while he talked about Sunaina. Zeba put a hand on Asif's shoulder to console him. They had lunch together and that evening both Asif and Zeba sat together during the gala dinner.

Zeba knew Rome well and suggested to Asif that the next day they meet at the Caffe Conti at Piazza Spagna. That night

Asif's thoughts revolved around Zeba. He remembered the five years spent in the Medical College when they had lived life as lovebirds. Was it an omen that they had met in Rome? He realised he was looking forward to meeting her next day.

Zeba couldn't believe that she would meet Asif again and that too in an alien setting. After Sidharth's death she had become lonely. On numerous occasions she thought she did not do the right thing to break from Asif. She remembered the long hours she and Asif would spend just walking in those chilly December nights. Her mind drifted to her first kiss. She felt she was counting hours when she was expected to meet Asif the next day.

Piazza Spagna was full of tourists that Saturday afternoon. Many tourists were throwing coins in the Fontana de Trevi and making fervent wishes. Zeba too threw a coin thinking of Asif. Last night she had slept very less, by the time she had dozed off she was already convinced that meeting Asif in Rome was an act of God. In between her remorse, her mind did remind her that it was she who had ditched Asif when he least expected. Zeba's mind thought of something. She decided to send a whatsapp message to Asif saying she was extremely sorry for her conduct six years back.

Asif woke up the next day with a heavy headache. Last night he dreamt of Sunaina. The dream revolved around Sunaina's last moments. She was asking him **'why did you marry me'.** As much as he thought of Zeba, he was reminded of Sunaina. Asif started hallucinating. In the empty room he heard the sound of Sunaina asking him **'why did you marry me'.** Asif called Air India and booked his flight back to India that afternoon. He packed his bag and called the radiotaxi for the airport.

Zeba took her seat at the Caffe Conti and waited. She

ordered a coffee and looked at her watch. It was just around 3 pm. She typed the sorry message which she had prepared last night and pressed the send button. She wanted to say sorry to Asif just before he came to meet her. Asif had already put his phone in flight mode. The air hostess was explaining the oxygen mask drill. The flight was airborne within five minutes.

# 7

## Shoot Out in Kamatipura

Her legs felt heavy and her body wanted her to stay for some more time in bed, she glanced at the wall clock, the two hands of the clock were juxtaposed, her groggy eyes tried to focus, it was on the third attempt while she lay lazily in bed that she looked towards the clock and realised it was five minutes to eleven. Her client last night had been extremely rough. With age not on her side, off late, she found it hard to coax her body to synchronize with the fantasy of her clients.

She wrapped the blanket and again turned on one side closing her eyes. Her mind meandered to thoughts which took her to her childhood; she realised an eon had passed in her life. Her mind went back to the memory of her hamlet in Jagdishpur where she had spent the first fifteen years of her life. She realised that her journey from Jagdishpur to the Kamatipura red light area of Mumbai had been extremely difficult and painful. In that moment of half-awake and half sleep, she momentarily forgot her present identity. Begam Jaan's mind transported her to the memory of her village house where as a girl she had gone to school and played with friends. Somewhere in a recess of her mind she came across a name which sounded familiar. A faint memory of someone addressing her as Seema filled her ears. In that moment when Begum Jaan's mind went into REM sleep, her neurons started conjuring images of her childhood, she started dreaming.

It was a winter morning and her mother was combing her hair. As her mother went about straightening her tresses, she put a shawl around Seema's exposed legs which were more than visible in that short frock. Seema had no idea what that trivial action meant but she did not object. She remembered that her mother had told her something about her appearance and how she must keep her body covered. Although Seema did not comprehend the exact meaning of her mother's monologue but she did understand that her mother had told her about some impending changes in her body. In veiled terms, mother had introduced some mention of periods, although Seema got no idea why her mother was saying all these things to her.

Seema's dream took her to a yet another etched episode of her life. It was the rainy season and with the leaking roof, she was huddled with her younger sister and mother in one corner of the room which doubled up as the living room, kitchen and the drawing room. Seema's mind played back the vivid memory of the moment when their father had come inside the room in a heavily inebriated state. The family was used to such episodes but on this rainy night something strange happened which had never happened before. Seema remembered the moment when her father had started groping her. Even in sleep this dream made her convulse. She opened her eyes. Her heart was beating fast. Begam Jaan breathed a sigh of relief when it dawned that she had been dreaming. She found the dream very disturbing. Her body was still sore from her unpleasant rough client last night. She wanted to sleep more. Her eyes drooped and she again went into slumber.

Her mind picked up her lost thoughts with ease as if her brief waking episode was just a hiccup in the unfolding story of her past. The next milestone which her mind stumbled upon was linked to her memories of the village school. Even at ten years, Seema had grown up to a physically endowed young girl. Her mother had time and again coaxed her to cover her bosom. Her dream took her to the times when she had started understanding that boys looked at her with a gaze which was weird. Ostensibly some boys would make veiled effort to brush past her.

Begam Jaan's dream was broken when someone gently prodded her asking why she had slept so long. She opened her eyes and glanced at the clock. Again, the two hands of the clock were juxtaposed, but this time on the other side of twelve. She realised it was five minutes past one. The dream sequence of the last couple of hours filled her mind with melancholy. Gingerly she got up and went to the bathroom.

The lingering after effects of the late morning dream continued to haunt Begam Jaan this afternoon. Her mind recollected her past story and she started to day dream. Her mind took her to that overcast cloudy day of July when she had reached her school but found that the school was closed due to rains. There were only a few people on the streets. In that drenched frock and leggings, she felt a bit embarrassed.

The three boys had forced her inside the school campus and took her to the isolated classroom. Her mouth was gagged. In the frenzy that followed for the next thirty minutes, Seema went through hell. The boys had run away leaving a bleeding Seema on the floor.

Begam Jaan wiped her tears which had swelled in her eyes. She wanted to stop her mind from playing more memories. She didn't want to remember the events which followed after she was taken home. In that fleeting memory, she remembered the humiliation of the police interrogation and the painful medical examination.

Her thoughts were broken and she returned to real time with the ringing of her mobile phone. She knew it was something important. Only a few people had access to her private number. The caller on the other side didn't need to introduce himself. He addressed her 'Jaan'. Begam Jaan was also at her polite best, despite being on a voice call; her countenance displayed the traditional etiquette of a seasoned courtesan engaged in the world's oldest profession. The caller on the other side of the virtual communication was the local MLA and the undisputed don of the area. He had long made it a habit not to take a 'no' as an answer. Begam Jaan knew if she had to run her business, she had to please Jabir. Whether it was due to power, terror or money, it hardly mattered, Begam Jaan said 'yes' and ended the conversation.

Begam Jaan closed her eyes and sighed. Tonight, she was in no mood to make herself available to a male lustful fantasy but her long association in the profession had made her understand that sex for a male was a double-edged sword. It could be both a reason for showering largesse or abuse. To make herself ready for tonight, she realised she needed a coffee.

The evening in the brothel was still a couple of hours away. Begam Jaan once again remembered her late morning dream which had taken her back to Jagdishpur. Although painful, the memories had after a long time opened a pandora's box. Begam Jaan's thoughts again went back to her story. She remembered how as a fifteen-year-old she had willingly submitted herself to the charm of her neighbour and eloped believing his promise of making it big in the tinsel world of

Bollywood. Her thoughts drifted to the time spent in dingy quarters of Byculla, Nagpara and Bhindi Bazaar. She lost count of how men would behave when they indulged in satisfying themselves. She also lost count of how many times her possession had changed in the hands of pimps and touts. Her racy mind finally stopped when the clock signaled nine. It was time to get ready for the night. Seema had finally got transformed into Begam Jaan.

The visitor was as discreet as a snake. Despite being covered by a high-profile personal security cover 24x7, Jabir chose to drive alone to reach the lane which housed the address of Begam Jaan. Privacy was an unsaid anthem in this part of the society; silently he was ushered in the secluded area where private rooms provided the perfect ambience for a night in the fantasy world. In her long career being part of the twilight industry, Begam Jaan had seen many a young or old, healthy or infirm and rich or pauper, seek emotional solace inside the dark alleys of Kamatipura. Tonight, she realised that Jabir was already past his prime. She harboured no qualms; Jabir was a spendthrift. In this aspect Jabir didn't disappoint this evening either, he paid handsomely. The visitor to Lane number 5, Kamatipura left before sunrise, as discretely as he had arrived.

The evening breeze from the sea was refreshing. Jabir sat on his favourite armchair and sipped coffee. His eyes scanned the far horizon where the Arabian sea met the blue skyline. Jabir's sea face Worli apartment was a prime location in Mumbai. With eyes aimlessly looking beyond the constant motion of the waves, his thoughts catapulted him to almost four decades back when as a teenager he had gone to a Christian Missionary convent school in Allahabad. Jabir's thoughts veered to the event which had changed his life. He remembered the afternoon when the henchmen of the local mafia don had pumped four bullets in the body of his father.

Involuntarily, Jabir clenched his fists. His mind continued to play out the sequence of events after his father's murder. The subsequent financial hardships, his induction in the world of crime, his first jail sentence, his first murder, the second jail sentence, his journey from Allahabad to Mumbai, and his initiation into the petty crimes in the underbelly of Mumbai. Even Jabir's mind found it hard to pinpoint how and when he had become the undisputed lord of the world of the crime. All these events flashed before his eyes in the form of a kaleidoscope of thoughts. Jabir's thoughts were punctuated by the opening of the gate on the ground floor. He saw his son drive the new BMW which was the gift of a doting father to his son on his twenty fifth birthday a few days back. The joy of seeing Salim melted Jabir's heart.

Since birth, Salim had seen opulence at home. In initial years of growing up Salim was sent to the best school in Mumbai. It was in college that Salim picked up drugs and started keeping company of boys who had no interest in studies. After a year in college, Salim had dropped out. Jabir had no time and probably no clear intent of counselling Salim. With easy money and all the luxuries already available, Jabir felt Salim had more than what was needed for the next two generations. A few days back Jabir had celebrated Salim's twenty fifth birthday with elan. Among other things, as part of the celebration, even Begam Jaan was invited for a dance performance. It was as a birthday gift that Jabir had presented Salim with a latest model of BMW.

In the last few years Salim had picked up the nuances of the criminal world. Although he was not directly involved in any of the activities of his father but the atmosphere in Jabir's house was sufficient enough to train Salim into the art of establishing criminal networks. Enchanted by the dance performance of Begam Jaan and attracted by her demeanor, Salim pulled a few strings to find out her address.

This Thursday morning had not started well for Jabir. In the wee hours of the morning, he received a cryptic message that his consignment of drugs being transported out of Mumbai had been intercepted by the police. Since morning Jabir had been on phone calling his contacts in the establishment to find a way out. It was the exigency of the moment that today he even forgot to take his morning medication for hypertension. The ensuing afternoon had also not gone too well. The news of losing out a few building contracts rattled him. He remembered that he had not met Salim for the whole day. Salim was his most prized life support. Sitting on his balcony, Jabir could see that Salim's new BMW was parked in the alley. Jabir thought Salim would be around.

Seven in the evening was like early morning in the lanes of Kamatipura. The real action always started late in the night. Despite the odd hour, few took notice to the taxi which had stopped at the door of the two storey house of Begam Jaan. The old man sporting a henna dyed beard knew too well that visitors needed to be escorted inside without any questions. Fifty years of experience in this trade was enough to make Naseem Mian understand that this visitor was some spoilt wealthy scion who was probably on his first visit to man's oldest recreational ground.

Begam Jaan had just finished her evening coffee. She overheard a few murmurs and without seeing the participants enquired in a loud voice seeking to know what was happening. In the next moment she was face-to-face with a young man, immaculately dressed and sporting a heavy gold chain. She recognised the visitor. She remembered it was just a week back when she had danced in the birthday party of this young man.

Despite her mind bringing back memories of her numerous episodes with Jabir, Begam Jaan's face showed no trace of disbelief. She behaved in her courteous best to offer the visitor a seat. Politely Salim stammered his desire to Begam Jaan. He offered an amount of money which was far more than what had ever been offered to Begam Jaan. Despite this offer, Begam Jaan made a few excuses. Salim was quick to offer her more. The temptation of money was just too large. Begam Jaan's mind went into overdrive exploring pros and cons. She reconciled that this young man would not take more than an hour. The prostitute's instinct in Begam Jaan took over, she said 'yes'.

Jabir felt lonely at home, the events of the day had drained him mentally. He contemplated to having a game of chess with Salim. Jabir remembered that he had not seen Salim since morning. He called Salim but his son's phone was not reachable, perhaps switched off. A tinge of anxiety crept into Jabir but he brushed aside any anxious thoughts, he consoled himself that it was still not late in the night, maybe Salim was with his friends. Jabir contemplated, he needed to relax after an emotionally sapping day, in an abstract gesture he picked up his phone and called 'Jaan'. Even Begam Jaan was not picking his call. Jabir found this weird because eight in the night was a safe time to call Begam Jaan. Despite not receiving any confirmation from Begam Jaan, Jabir decided to visit her this evening.

Begum Jaan escorted Salim to the privacy of her room. Salim was quick to take off his clothes. Begam Jaan found the energy and the excitement of Salim both infectious and amusing. He was so different from his father. Begam Jaan realised that after a long time, she too found a sense of intense gratification in the act. Time flew fast without any pause, both

Salim and Begam Jaan lost count of the time spent in each other's company.

Jabir met Naseem Mian at the door and was surprised to be greeted with a queer countenance. Jabir was escorted inside the house but was ushered in a room which was not the usual meeting place with Begam Jaan. When Begam Jaan did not come out for the next fifteen minutes, Jabir felt a bout of anger. Time passed and his anger grew pronounced. Suddenly he stood up and decided to go inside the house where he usually spent time with Begam Jaan. With Naseem Mian doing his best to restrain Jabir from going inside, Jabir nonchalantly walked down the corridor and reached the room where he had spent numerous nights in the company of Begam Jaan.

The animated conversation between Jabir and Naseem Mian also reached Begam Jaan while she lay exhausted and overwhelmed with a perspiring Salim within skin distance. Someone was banging at the door. The banging grew intense and suddenly the latch got released. In that moment of frenzy, Begam Jaan threw the blanket across the naked body of Salim. Jabir, in rage, was hurling expletives. He whipped out his revolver and fired twice at the companion lying next to Begam Jaan. Begam Jaan was dazed, she opened her mouth to say something but no words escaped her lips. Without saying anything, Jabir silently got to his car and returned.

A commotion had broken in Begam Jaan's house. The unexplained shoot out and a murder were something which needed police intervention. Begam Jaan knew that the murder of Salim by Jabir would be too hot for the police and the underworld. She realized something needed to be done. She dialed a few numbers from her personal mobile, one of them being the private number of the highest police officer. Even in the confines of her room, Begam Jaan covered her mouth to shield her conversation lest somebody overheard it.

Within an hour, an ambulance silently made its way in the lane and parked in front of the house. The body was wheeled inside the ambulance under the supervision of two policemen. The ambulance retreated as discretely as it had arrived.

Doctor Salman was getting ready to finish his emergency duty at the Byculla General Hospital when he received a call. The call was from someone who commanded lot of respect, even while receiving the call Doctor Salman started by saying 'Yes Sir'. The man on the other side gave some instructions. No other words were exchanged. A drained Doctor Salman changed his route, he silently walked towards the mortuary.

The body lying on the barren stone slab was of a twenty-five-year-old male, strongly built and fair. Two bullet wounds were clearly visible, one on the chest and the other on the stomach. The doctor made a long incision on the body starting from the neck upto the stomach. Without peering inside, he made a few stiches and closed the open skin. Doctor Salman retreated to his chamber within five minutes. The post mortem report signed by the medical officer stated that the twenty-five-year-old male body bearing the police tag 'Salim' had died of heart attack.

It was at the stroke of ten in the night that Jabir received a call from the Police Commissioner. Jabir looked stunned. He stammered on the phone. The man who had last wept almost fifty years back when he had seen his father's death body, wept again. He heard a faint siren of the ambulance on the road outside his house. His eyes fell on the table where the chess men were arranged neatly on sixty-four black and white squares. He remembered the almost daily after dinner routine when he would play a game of chess with Salim.